THE ROCK PLUNGED INTO ETERNITY

ALBA HOUSE BOOKS BY ARCHBISHOP FULTON J. SHEEN

The Divine Romance

The Eternal Galilean

Guide to Contentment

The Prodigal World

The Seven Capital Sins

The Seven Last Words

You

Way to Inner Peace

Way to Happiness

Vist our web site at
WWW.ALBAHOUSE.ORG
or call 1-800-343-2522 (ALBA)
and request current catalog

The Rock Plunged Into Eternity

FULTON J. SHEEN, PhD, DD

Agrégé en Philosophie de L'Université de Louvain and
The Catholic University of America

ST PAULS

Alba House

Originally printed and distributed by Our Sunday Visitor,
Huntington, Indiana for the National Council of Catholic Men

Library of Congress Cataloging-in-Publication Data

Sheen, Fulton J. (Fulton John), 1895-1979.
  The rock plunged into eternity / Fulton J. Sheen.
    p. cm.
  ISBN 0-8189-0952-8
  1. Meditations. 2. Christian life—Catholic authors. I. Title.

BX2182.3.S53 2003
252'.02—dc21

                                        2003004204

Imprimatur:
✠ John Francis Noll, D.D.
Bishop of Fort Wayne

ISBN: 0-8189-0952-8

Eighteen addresses delivered in the nationwide Catholic Hour,
produced by the National Council of Catholic Men, in cooperation with
the National Broadcasting Company, from January 1, 1950 through
April 9, 1950.

This Alba House edition is produced by special arrangement with the
Estate of Fulton J. Sheen and the Society for the Propagation of the
Faith, 366 Fifth Avenue, New York, NY 10001. It has been revised to
incorporate a more recent and more recognizable translation of the
Scripture texts.

This book is published in the United States of America
by Alba House, the publishing arm of the Society of St. Paul,
an international religious congregation of priests and brothers
serving the Church through the communications media.

Printing Information:

Current Printing - first digit   1   2   3   4   5   6   7   8   9   10

Year of Current Printing - first year shown

2004   2005   2006   2007   2008   2009   2010   2011   2012

A special word of thanks to the
Oblates of Mary Immaculate
Lesmurdie, Western Australia
and the
Fulton J. Sheen Society of Perth Western Australia, Inc.
for having encouraged the publication of this book
and provided us with the text of this fine work.

TABLE OF CONTENTS

THE ROCK PLUNGED INTO ETERNITY

LOVE ONE ANOTHER

ADDRESS DELIVERED ON JANUARY 1, 1950

"Love your enemies, do good to those who hate you, pray for those who persecute and insult you, that you may be true sons and daughters of your Father in heaven."
(Luke 6:28 and Matthew 5:44)

Friends:

Happy New Year! May God bless all your comings and goings! May you give to God each day of the New Year, the three things which He has not in His Infinite Treasury: your need of Him, your wants, and your contrition for sin.

The best way to start a broadcast is with love, not only for those who love us, but for those who do not! I firmly believe that there are only two classes of people in the world: those who have found God, and those who are looking for Him. From the viewpoint of love, there are no persecutors, bigots or scoffers. They are just so many souls to love. And so our initial broadcast will be to invite you to take all three to your heart's embrace.

Persecutors. First consider the persecutors! Despite the fact that there are probably more martyrs for the faith since 1917, than during two hundred and fifty years of the Roman persecution; despite the fact that in this evil hour, Hungarian and Polish and other priests are being crucified to the walls of their rectories, we still must love our persecutors with a Christ-like love.

Penetrate the mystery of this persecution. Suppose those persecutors who call themselves the enemies of God, left us alone or ignored us; and suppose it made no difference to them whether we loved Christ and Him Crucified. This would be a sign that our salt had lost its savor, that our fires had gone out, and that our lips were no longer touched by Heaven's coals. It used to be that the character of people was known by those who loved them; today characters are better known by those who hate them. If racketeers hate the judges of our courts, this is a tribute to their justice. Whenever the wicked hate the souls that are in love with Our Dear Lord, this is a sign of how much they know that your love of Christ spells doom to their evil ways. The persecutors know that the only thing that stands in the way of Communism conquering the world is the love of our hearts for Christ's Mystical Body. (If you wish to know what is Christ's Mystical Body I refer you to St. Paul. If you prefer to wait, I will tell you in a few weeks.) The persecutors are paying us the beautiful tribute of hostility, the fine compliment of opposition. The egotists and the indifferent in our land never think about Our Lord, or our holy faith, or the Divine Presence on our altars. But the persecutors do. They know that if Christ's love continued in His Mystical Body prevails, they are doomed. But never forget that we too must pray for them as Our Savior did for His persecutors: "Father, forgive them, for they know not what they do." Our Lord told us that these unhappy days would come, and bade us be happy in them. "Blessed are you when men hate you and exclude you and insult you, when they reject your name as evil on account of the Son of Man. Rejoice on that day and leap for joy; for behold, your reward will be great in heaven." (Luke 6:33)

Please God, a day will come when those who persecute will love, for hate is nothing but love upside down. Every day say a prayer for Russia. If it is not brought to God, it will continue to spread wars and revolutions throughout the world. If it is brought to God, it will become one of the greatest witnesses to His Divine Son on the face of the earth. It may interest you to know, that every day I use in the Holy Sacrifice of the Mass, a Chalice that was made in Russia and which was once used by the priests of that country. The Russian Communists sold it to a Jewish friend of mine who, knowing of my spiritual interest in the Russian people, gave me the Chalice in order that it might be used to offer

Calvary's Sacrifice for the intention of Russia. It is my fondest wish that some day when peace and the love of God come back again to Russia, the Chalice will be restored to those people and that they may pray for us as we now pray for them. They are not as far away from Our Lord as some of our indifferent men of the Western World. The Communist soldier who shot at a host during a procession of the Blessed Sacrament, would not shoot at a loaf of bread. He *knew* the difference, even in his act of violence. He believes in the Real Presence but not yet to adore. Even now the Russians in concentration camps are singing the old Cossack song:

> "Siberia is conquered to Christ
> And we have not lived in vain."

Grant, O Heart of Jesus that they may quickly return to the Father's house, and make their fires that now burn downward *in hate,* burn upward in love of Thy Holy Name.

Bigots. Love also those who are called bigots. We do not like the term, because it is narrow; from this point on we shall designate them as "friends." Many of them are well-intentioned and say evil things against our Lord's Mystical Body only out of ignorance. Should we expect to be immune from lies, when Our Lord Himself was accused of politically perverting the nation? At least there is this consolation; they have to think about Christ's Mystical Body in order to attack it. They do not write or preach against Mars, because they do not think about Mars. Psychology teaches us that such a hatred is born of the fear of loving. Maybe the reason they want to *talk* so much about the Mystical Body of Christ is because for the moment they are afraid to *hear* about it. But give them time. They are really fighting a love of it, as Paul did when he held the garments of those who stoned Stephen; and yet St. Paul became one of the greatest Apostles of Christ's Mystical Body.

Furthermore, if you and I had been brought up on the same lies that these good people have been told, we would probably hate the Body of Christ a thousand times more than they do. They really do not hate it; they only hate what they mistakenly believe to be the Body of Christ. It is of course a pity that those men who profess to serve the cause of Christ and who wear the vesture of religion, should spread hatred and lies about their neighbors in other faiths who are also trying to serve Him. There is already too much hate, envy, jealousy and slander in our world. How much better it would be, if those who *say* they speak in the Name of God, would only try to make everyone *love* God. Plumbers do not smash pipes, but repair them. Men of religion ought to diffuse love, not hate and dissension.

Would to God those of us who profess to love

the Mystical Body as we do, thought as much about it, wrote as much about it, preached as much about it as do these good people. They are serving the cause of Our Lord unwittingly, for they are waking up people to a realization that the Rock is something that makes a difference. (I am using the word Rock as Our Lord did in Matthew 16:18.)

It is not for us to judge these people. They must be left to God. They have passion and fire, and God can do something with them which He cannot do with the tepid. The latter, He said, He would vomit from His Mouth. If Our Lord did not love them, He never would have chosen Paul, who was one of the greatest of the bigots! I firmly believe that when the day comes, through penance and devotion to the Immaculate Heart of Mary for the regeneration of the world, our greatest apostles and saints will come not so much from us who are tepid, as from those whose fires God can use to illumine a world! Regardless of what they say against Christ's Mystical Body, love them, pray for them, be kind to them, that you may be children of your Father Who is in Heaven.

Finally, *Mockers*. They too, we call "friends." Here we make a special plea to those of you who have the fullness of faith grounded on the Rock. You complain that people heckle and annoy you because of your faith, as they called Our Lord a wine-biber and a glutton. You protest that they ask you all kinds of questions, not because they want an answer, but because they do not. That is good! Thank God for it! They never sneer at anyone else, no matter what his creed, even though it be his own invention. These they leave absolutely alone. But they ridicule and harrass you, because they know that you have something which they have not, and because your faith is a reproach to evil. In the back of their heads they wish they had *your* peace; they would like *your* certitude instead of their doubts, *your* joy instead of their fears, and *your* trust in God instead of their confusion. They envy you and want what you have, but they want it at their price, not Christ's. In a word, they want your faith without a Cross.

Can you not see that they are on the defensive? Have you ever noticed how many of them are writing and talking and giving reasons why they *do not* believe in Christ's Mystical Body? Nobody asked them for their reasons; nobody invited them to build their little house on the Rock; but they feel bound to tell you why they are not doing it. Nobody goes around telling people why they are not believers in a new Sun Cult or why "Paint the Barn Week" is a snare invented by a paint manufacturer. This is because people are not conscious of Sun Cults and barns. But all of a sudden, these people have become conscious that they do not have the faith, so they immediately proceed to justify their position. The Chinese who come to this country never lecture on why they are not Confucianists, but these Confusionists have to tell us why they are against our faith. They never tell us *what they believe,* but what they do *not* believe. They never give a lecture on why they go to Rock Island, but they give profuse lectures on why they never go to the Rock.

Understand the psychology of these good people and be patient with them. Whenever you hear anyone attacking belief in God, the Moral Law, the Divinity of Christ and His Mystical Body, remember this rule: Never consider so much what people say, but *why* they say it. Some objections come not from their reason but from their behavior or the way they live. They are protesting, arguing against, or even sneering, because they have an urge to do something about the thing which they are fighting. No mother ever told a son not to go near the water, if the son did not have an urge to go swimming. These people may not be in love with anything Divine, but they are unconsciously afraid that they may fall in love with Our Lord because there is so much to admire.

All of a sudden the world has become filled with a race of people called the "I am not." Our Divine Lord seven times said "I am," e.g., "I am the Good Shepherd"; 70x7 these people say: "I am not," e.g. "I am not a believer because." Their words tell how empty they are and how they hunger for the Eucharistic Bread that makes us one. They talk as if they were disappointed in love — and everyone is who has only the world to love. That is why they warn everyone against falling in love with Christ's Mystical Body. Like a man who missed the boat, they tell others never to go to sea for a rest. They admit their thirst, but they do not want others to drink.

These people are looking for Truth. And Truth has left the universities and the press and has entered into the bread we eat, the work we do, the agonies we suffer, the satieties we feel, the sense and apprehension of the atomic bomb, the fear of living, the emptiness of pleasure, the solitariness of lying awake at night. *God is coming* to these souls, not through their reason which is weak, but through their hunger which is great. If we fail to understand the way their hearts work, we will drive them from God. Their mockery and their sneers are only masks, which in their hearts they want us to see through. They are to be less censured than those of us, who hate them because they hate us. Be charitable to them! You would not turn a starving man from your door, even though he insulted you; much less should we turn away a hungry heart. Realize the blessings that you have, the doubts from which you are saved, the false hates from which you have escaped, and how dark your mind would be if it were not illumined by faith. Praise God that He has given you this insight and these Sacraments which pour the Christ-Life into your soul. Think of those who would love the Rock more than you, who would be more frequent in Communion with Our Lord if they had your faith; who would be more zealous with the Truth, more charitable with their hands, and more kindly with their lips.

Millions there are who are fluttering like wounded birds around the Rock. Get on your knees for them; sacrifice for them. Be the sign of the Eternal on the face of the earth, the mystery of Faith against the mystery of iniquity. Bear love to those who hate; bring pity to the world's tears; bless those who have forgotten the need of blessing. Be the hidden writing on the parchment of their world. Be the stars of their dark nights.

If *you* are silent for a day, some light in the world will fail, *some soul* must spend the night in darkness. Be not alone in your happiness, or it shall be taken away. *You* believe in God! The time is coming now when these poor frustrated souls will realize there is no one else in whom they can believe. The alternative to God is not man; it is the Devil! This is becoming clearer every day to every man.

Fold your fingers like Gothic spires into a carnal decade of your Rosary. Forgive those who persecute, love those who hate, bless those who sneer! This is *Our Lord's* way, and we cannot be worthy of Him unless we follow Him. Who is the stronger, I ask you: The one who says "If you will not love me, then I will hate you," or the one who says: "Even though you hate me, I will always love you." If any drop of our love ever changed into hate, it would prove that it was never love from the beginning, for love is as changeless as God!

If you go into the world with the idea that everyone is an enemy or a bigot you will be surprised how many enemies and bigots you will meet. But if you go into the world with the assurance that everyone is looking for Our Lord, you will be surprised how many lovable people you meet. I am meeting them everywhere. Plant love where you do not find it, and everyone will be lovable!

God love you!

THE ETERNAL CHRIST
THROUGH THE CENTURIES

ADDRESS DELIVERED ON JANUARY 8, 1950

*"Friends, I will not leave you orphaned; I am
coming to you."*   (John 14:17)

Friends:

"Give me a man who loves and I will tell him what
God is." Such are the words of St. Augustine. Anyone who ever loved craved unity with that which he
loved. Thus in marriage the ideal is the unity of two
in one flesh; in religion the ideal is to be one with
Christ. There is not a single person who loves Our
Dear Lord, who does not strive to be united to Him
in thought and in desire and even in body and mind.
But here is the problem: How be one with Christ?

His earthly life ended over nineteen hundred
years ago. Therefore to some He is only a Figure
Who crossed the stage of history, as did Caesar and
Aristotle, and then is seen no more. Such souls believe that the *only way* they can be united with Our
Lord, is by reading what someone wrote concerning Him, or by singing hymns in His Name, or by

listening to a sermon on His Life.

It is no wonder that such people soon begin to think of Our Lord as a teacher of ethics, or as a great humanitarian reformer like Buddha or Socrates, for they too also once lived, preached and edified and left behind them a beautiful memory. It is only minds with little power of penetration who say that Our Dear Lord "was a good man." May I say that this is precisely what Our Lord was not, viz., a good man, because good men do not lie. If He is not what He claimed to be, what His miracles witnessed, what the Jewish and Gentile prophecies foretold, viz., the Son of the Living God — then He is not just a good man. Then He is a liar, a knave, a deceiver, and a charlatan. If He is not the Christ, the Son of the Living God, He is the anti-Christ; but He is not just a good man.

Let us try to understand what Our Divine Lord really is. Begin with yourself. Have you ever thought of how wonderfully you have been made; that there is in you something which can be seen and touched, namely your body whose nature is flesh; but there is also something invisible about you, namely your mind and soul with its thoughts, its loves and its desires. Your soul is, in a sense, "incarnate" in a body (the word incarnate, as you know, means in the flesh), that is, your soul animates and unifies your body.

Now consider the Person of Our Divine Lord.

He is the true incarnation, not of a soul in a body, but of God in the form of man. There is something visible about Him, namely, His perfect human nature, which can handle tools, pat little children's heads, be thirsty and think and desire like other men. But there is also something invisible about Him, and that is His Divinity. His Divinity could no more be seen than your soul, though it could be seen working through His human nature, as your soul works through your body. Just as your body and your soul combine to make one person, so in an infinitely more perfect way, His human nature and His Divine Nature make but one person, the Person of Jesus Christ, the Son of the Living God, true God and true man.

We are now prepared to reread our Gospels. St. John closes His Gospel with the words that if he had written down all Our Lord had done "the world itself would not be able to contain the books that should be written" (John 21:25). This beautiful variety of Our Lord's words and actions however, can be reduced to three: He taught, He governed and He sanctified. He taught, because He is Teacher; He governed, because He is King; He sanctified because He is Savior or Priest.

First, as Teacher, He is Truth. Because He is God, He is absolutely Divine infallible Truth. He said: "I am the Truth." For the first time in history, Truth and Personality were identified. Up until then

and since, men have always said: "Here is my doctrine; this is my system; follow these rules." But these
ideals were outside their personality, just mere ab-
stractions. No man can fall in love with a theory of
geometry or a metaphysical proposition. Truth to
be loved must be personal and Our Lord pointed
to Himself as the Truth. No one else ever taught that
He was the personification of Truth. Buddha and
others gave systems apart from their personalities.
But in the Person of Our Lord, Truth and Personality were one. There was no Truth apart from Him.
He *is* the Truth. Hence, those who say "the beati-
tudes are the core of His Teaching" miss the point.
There was nothing recommended or taught outside
or beyond Him, for in Him all the scattered ways
and systems found their center and their source.
Everyone else gave a code, but He is as romantic as
love. All Truth — philosophic, scientific, artistic,
and legal — is in Him. He is Wisdom. He is all the
arts and all the sciences. He is the University, for all
knowledge turns about Him Who is the Truth with
Whom we can fall in love.

Do you really believe that this Divine Truth
would come to this earth, speak a few words, and
allow them to be wafted away by a Galilean breeze?
It is absurd to believe that He Who wrote only once
in His Life, and that was in the sands, and Who
never told anyone to write, should have intended
that His Truth should be available only and exclu-

sively in a few memoranda that were written down by a few followers over twenty years after His Death, and were never gathered together in their approved form until three centuries later? Grant that they are inspired and revealed, and I believe it and confess it and read those writings daily; but I still say it is unthinkable that these books which were not written until His Mystical Body was already spread throughout the whole Roman Empire, should be *His only way* of communicating Truth. If He did not take some effective guarantee to preserve His Truth, which was so sacred that He died for it, then Truth did not matter to Him. If He could not prolong His Truth, up to this hour, then He is not God. Either that infallible Truth of Jesus Christ is living now, available now, or He is not God. Our problem is to find that infallible Divine Truth. Come, O Christ, not with a dead Truth, but with a living, breathing, speaking Truth which is the Truth of God to lead the world from darkness into the light. Come with it, even though You have to use human nature to communicate it now as You did then.

Secondly, Our Lord fulfilled the office of King. As King He is the source of authority. There is something else beside His Truth that He ought to have communicated, and that is His Authority. As the Son of God He said: "All authority in Heaven and on earth has been given to Me" (Matthew 28:18). The winds and the seas obeyed Him, and when Pilate boasted that he had the power to condemn Him (dictators always speak that way), Our Lord reminded him: "You would have no power over Me at all, if it had not been given you from above" (John 19:11).

It is absolutely incredible that this Power to change the hearts of all nations should have died with Our Lord. We are living in a world where false authorities are claiming our allegiance, where public opinion makes us dizzy; where the power of the State invades all personal rights. Hence we have need of someone to remind the modern Pilates that there is another Power from above. We have plenty of authorities to tell us what is right when the world is right; we want a living Christ today who will tell us what is right when the world is wrong. Come, O Christ, with Your Divine Authority, make us free, even though You have to use human natures now as You used a human nature then.

Thirdly, Our Lord fulfilled the office of Priest or Redeemer, for He is the Author of our sanctification. When Our Blessed Lord was on earth, not only did He lift up limbs long paralyzed with disease and death, and open blind eyes to the light of God's sunshine, but He cleansed souls and purged hearts. As He identified Truth and Power with His Personality, so He identified Sanctification: "I am the Life." And by Life, He did not mean mere physical life, but spiritual, sanctified, divinized life. He came as a link between God and man. Man is unholy; God is holy, and there is nothing in common between the two. But because He is both God and man, therefore He could be mediator between earth and Heaven. This is the meaning of Christ the Priest, a link between God and man, bringing God to man and man to God.

It is absurd to think that God Who came to this earth to forgive sins, sanctify our souls and elevate us to a higher life, should have left us to the mercy of a few literary records and a few hymns to attain this Divine Life. Shall the Magdalens of our streets be denied the forgiveness that came to the woman who entered Simon's house? Shall the frustrated, the bored, the alcoholics, the fearful who are the way they are because of their sins, go on unforgiven because Christ forgot to prolong His forgiving power? Shall they whose minds are burdened because they cannot be detached from the past, suffer the added agony of thinking that Christ is past and gone?

Some think, for this reason, that Our Lord should have remained on earth. But Our Lord knew better. In answer to such a request, He said: "It is better for you that I go. For if I do not go, the Advocate (He Who is to befriend you) will not come to you" (John 16:7). He is saying that if He remained on earth, we could never get any closer to Him than the touch of a hand, or the sound of a voice, or the thrill of an embrace, which is far below the degree of intimacy that God wants with the soul, and the soul desires with God. But if He ascended into Heaven and sent to us His Spirit, then He would not be an example to be copied, but a veritable life to be lived. Then His Mind would be our mind; His Life, our life.

This much is *certain*. We who live nineteen hundred years after His birth should not be penalized for this accident of time and space. It may very well be that we have more need of Him now, than did the people of His time. I should be very much inclined to doubt His Divinity if He could not overcome the barriers of years and boundaries of space, and make the great gifts which He brought to Galilee and Judea available to London, New York and Moscow; to the shepherds of Texas as well as Bethlehem, and to the fishermen of Massachusetts as Capernaum.

If Christ is only the memory of someone who lived and suffered and died and who has left us orphans, then it is better to abandon Him. If Christianity is only the memory of some man who taught, governed and sanctified nineteen hundred years ago, and then left us only a few records written by other men, then the sooner we forget it the quicker we can begin our search for the Divine.

But Christ *does live*. He said that: "I shall be with you all days even to the consummation of the world." Our problem is to find out where and how He lives today. This is not hard. We begin with the fact that He first taught, governed and sanctified *through* a human nature which was given to Him by His Mother who was overshadowed by the Holy Spirit. He *taught* through that Body Mary gave Him; He governed through the Body that Mary nursed; He sanctified through the Body that Mary offered on the Cross for the Redemption of the world.

This being so, I would not be at all surprised if that is not the way He will continue to live through the centuries, namely, in another Body; this time not a physical and individual Body like the one He took from Mary, but in a social and mysterious Body such as He might take from the womb of humanity, and overshadow it with the same Holy Spirit. Thus as He taught, governed and sanctified through His *physical* Body, so He will continue to teach, govern and sanctify through a social Body which He would infuse with His Spirit and which He would govern as its Head. If He ever sent His Spirit to it, then it would be a Mystical Body.

This desire to be one with Christ cannot be satisfied with sermons, books and hymns. I can hear you say if He is only a memory, I do not want Him. I know what I do not want, and I know what I want. *I do not want* a dead truth spoken centuries ago. What is written in your books, in your Aristotles, and your Platos, can satisfy only for an hour. I want a living, breathing Truth with a tongue. I want a Power and Authority over me that treats the subjects as sheep and lambs, and to whom no authority is given until he who is to enjoy it, says to You three times, in the words of Peter: O Christ, I love You, I love You, I love You.

I want to be better in the sense of being sanctified, and I know that psychology cannot make me better because I am only lifting myself with my own bootstraps. I want no sanctification that is just a warm feeling down in the pit of my stomach. I want forgiveness of my sins, *now*. I want Your Life, O Christ, in my body and in my blood: I want the living Divine Presence in me, so that I do not live, but rather You, O Christ, live in me. I am human enough, too human; I want to be made a partaker of Your Divinity. This alone is sanctification.

I am sure, O Christ, that I shall find You, my Teacher, my King and my Priest. I know that somewhere You still teach and govern and sanctify, and I shall not rest until I find Your Body among men. I want no organization standing between You and me; I want nothing that started yesterday afternoon or a thousand years ago and that boasts it speaks in Your Name. I want You! Absolute Truth, Living Authority, Divine Life! And when I do find You, I shall never let You go! And You, O Eternal Christ, living through the centuries, when I find You, hold me fast, that I may never leave You!

I know through Your Gift of Faith where Your Body is and what it is. If there are any in the radio audience, O Christ, who would like to know where it is, inspire them to listen next Sunday!

THE MYSTICAL BODY OF CHRIST

ADDRESS DELIVERED ON JANUARY 15, 1950

"And behold I am with you always until the consummation of the world." (Matthew 28:20)

Friends:

If you asked me the three things we must have to be happy, I would say:

1. A Wisdom beyond all the partial knowledge of earth.
2. A Power greater than either man alone or man in society.
3. A Love that would die if need be, to save us if we failed.

These three we said last Sunday are in Christ, Who is Infallible Truth; Divine Power or Authority; and Heavenly Love or Holiness.

But we also said that His Truth is no more Divine than Buddha's if it is available only in a few fragments written by men after His Death; that His Power and Authority is no more Divine than

Lincoln's if it is available only in a few biographies; and His Love is no more heavenly than that of Socrates if we cannot have our sins forgiven now by Him, as did Magdalene and the penitent thief. Then if He did not prolong His Truth, His Authority, His Holiness, to us then He is not good. If He could not, then He is not God.

But He is God, and He did provide to make His Truth, Authority and Life available to us in this century. But how? In the same way He did then; through human nature. When you write, you use your hand as the visible instrument of your invisible mind; so He, Who is God, in a more perfect way, taught, governed, and sanctified through His human nature, which was the visible instrument of His Invisible Divinity. In plain language, you would have seen His Body; but you would have heard, obeyed, and been forgiven by God in Christ.

Our Lord said that He would take on a New Body, and that through it He would continue to be united with us until the end of time. It would not be another physical Body like that which He took from Mary. That human nature is now glorified at the right hand of His Father. He spoke of another kind of Body. If you look up the word "body" in the dictionary, you will find it can mean one of two things: either something physical or something social, i.e., either a physical organism of flesh and blood which is vivified by a soul; or it can mean a social grouping of persons who are considered as a whole because they have the same ideals and help one another. For example, we speak of the nation as the "body politic," or of a group of university professors as an "educational body." This New Body would not be like these, i.e., a *moral* body, for their unity comes from the will of men. Rather His New Social Body would be bound to Him not by the will of men, but by His Heavenly Spirit which He would send on leaving this earth.

Here are only seven of the many things He said about His Social Body which He would assume:

1. He told us that to be a member of His New Body we would have to be born into it. But it would not be through a *human* birth, for that only makes us sons of Adam; to be a member of His New Body we would have to be reborn through the Spirit in the waters of Baptism which would make us children of God.

2. The unity between this New Body and Him would not be through singing hymns to him, or having social teas in His Name, or listening to broadcasts, but through sharing His Life: "I am the Vine, you are its branches.... Live on in Me, and I will live on in you" (John 15:5, 4).

3. His New Body would be like all living things, small at first — even, as He said: "like a mustard seed," but it would grow from simplicity to complexity until the consummation of the world.

As He put it: "first the blade, then the ear, then the full grain in the ear" (Mark 4:28, 29).

4. A house expands from the outside in, by the addition of brick to brick; human organizations grow by the addition of man to man, i.e., from the circumference to the center. His Body, He said, would be formed from the inside out, like a living embryo is formed in the human body. As He received Life from the Father, we would receive Life from Him. As He put it: "That they may all be one, as You, Father, are in Me and I in You" (John 17:21).

5. Our Lord said that He would have only one Body. It would be a spiritual monstrosity for Him to have many bodies, or a dozen heads. To keep it one, it would have one Shepherd whom He said would feed His lambs and His sheep. "There will be one fold, and one shepherd" (John 10:16).

6. He said that His New Body would not manifest itself before men until the day of Pentecost when He would send His Truth-giving Spirit. "He will not come to you unless I do go" (John 16:7). Anything that would start therefore, even 24 hours after Pentecost, or 24 hours ago would be an organization all right; it might have the human spirit, but it would not have the Divine Spirit; it would be like an electric wire that was not connected to a dynamo.

7. The most interesting observation He made about His Body was that it would be hated by the world, as He was. Anything worldly, the world

loves. But what is Divine, the world hates. "Because I have chosen you out of the world, the world hates you" (John 15:20).

The nucleus of this New Social Body was to be His Apostles. They were to be the raw material into which He would send His Spirit to quicken them into His prolonged Self. They would represent Him when He was gone. The privilege of evangelizing the world was reserved to them. This New Body, of which they were the embryo, was to be His Posthumous Self, and His prolonged Personality, through the centuries.

Here we come to something really startling! Remember Our Lord is Teacher, King, and Priest or Savior. But now we find Him communicating to His New Body, His triple office of teaching, governing and sanctifying. He Who is the infallible Teacher and Who said: "I am the Truth," now tells His Body "I will send… the Truth-giving Spirit, to guide you in all Truth" (John 16:13). So much would He be identified with the New Body, that when anyone heard His Body speak, they would be hearing Him. "Whoever listens to you, listens to Me; whoever rejects you, rejects Me; and whoever rejects Me, rejects the One Who sent Me" (Luke 10:16). His Truth would be the Body's Truth — and therefore infallible, Divine Heavenly Truth.

Secondly, Our Lord Who is King, said: "All authority in Heaven and on earth has been given to

Me" (Matthew 28:18). This authority He so communicates to His Body that *their* commands are *His* commands; *their* orders are *His* orders which He ratifies: "Amen, I say to you, whatever you bind on earth shall be bound in Heaven, and whatever you loose on earth, shall be loosed in Heaven" (Matthew 18:18).

Finally, Our Lord is Priest or Mediator, for He redeemed us for God through His Death on the Cross. This Holiness and Power of sanctification He now communicates to His Body. His Body is told to baptize, to offer the Memorial of His Death, and — oh! what a blessed gift! — to forgive sins. "Whose sins you forgive *are forgiven* them, and whose sins you retain are retained" (John 20:23).

The nucleus of this Social Body we said was the Apostles. But until Our Lord sent His Spirit on them fifty days after His Resurrection, they were like the elements in a chemical laboratory. We know up to one hundred percent the chemicals which enter into the constitution of a human body, but we cannot make a baby because we lack the unifying principle of a soul. The Apostles could not give their Body Divine Life any more than chemicals can make human life. They needed God's invisible, Divine Spirit to unify their visible human natures.

Accordingly, ten days after the Ascension, the Glorified Savior Who is in Heaven sends upon them His Spirit, not in the form of a Book, but as tongues of living fire. As cells in a body form a new human life when God breathes a soul into the embryo, so the Apostles appeared as the visible Body of Christ when the Holy Spirit came to make them one. This is called in Tradition and Scripture the "whole Christ" or "the fulness of Christ."

The New Body of Christ now appears publicly before men. Just as the Son of God took upon Himself a human nature from the womb of Mary, overshadowed by the Holy Spirit, so now He takes a New Body from the womb of humanity, overshadowed by the Holy Spirit. Just as He once taught, governed and sanctified through human nature, so now He continues to teach, to govern, and to sanctify through other human natures which make up His Body.

Because this Body is not *physical* like a man, nor moral like a bridge club, but heavenly and spiritual because of the Spirit which made it one, it is called a Mystical Body. As my body is made up of millions and millions of cells, and yet is one because vivified by one soul, presided over by one visible head and governed by an invisible mind, so this New Body of Christ, though made up of millions and millions of persons who are incorporated into Christ by Baptism, is one because it is vivified by the Holy Spirit of God, and presided over by one visible head and governed by one invisible Mind or Head Who is the Risen Christ.

This Mystical Body is His prolonged Self! That

He is continuing to live in it now, recall the story of St. Paul whose Hebrew name was Saul. Perhaps no one ever lived who hated Christ more than Saul. The early members of Christ's Mystical Body prayed that God would send someone to refute him. God heard their prayer; He sent Paul to answer Saul. One day this persecutor, breathing with hatred, set out on a journey to Damascus to seize the members of Christ's Mystical Body there and bind them and bring them back to Jerusalem. The time was only a few years after the Ascension of Our Divine Savior. Remember that Our Lord is now glorified in Heaven. Suddenly a great light shone about Saul and he fell to the ground. Aroused by a Voice like a bursting sea he hears: "Saul, Saul, why are you *persecuting Me?*" Nothingness dared to ask the Name of Omnipotence: "Who are You, Lord?" And the Voice answered: "I am Jesus Whom you are persecuting."

How could Saul be persecuting Our Lord Who is now glorified in Heaven? Saul was doing nothing that Stalin is not now doing to Poland and Hungary. Why then should the Voice from Heaven say: "Saul, Saul, why are you persecuting Me?"

Well if someone stepped on your foot, would not your head complain because it is part of your body? Our Lord is now saying that in striking His Body, Saul is striking Him. When the Body of Christ is persecuted, it is Christ the Invisible Head Who arises to speak and to protest.

The Mystical Body of Christ therefore no more stands between Christ and me, than His physical Body stood between Magdalene and His forgiveness, or His Hand stood between the little children and His Blessing. It was through His human Body that He came to men in His individual Life; it is through His Mystical Body that He comes to us in His mystical corporate Life. Christ is living now! He is teaching now, governing now, sanctifying now. He has His glorious moments in other Palm Sundays; His scandalous moments of history when other Judases betray Him; and His suffering moments as He has now in His Stepinacs and Mindszentys and Berans, who are also "suffering under Pontius Pilate."

If you asked me what the Body of Christ means to me, I would say: "I believe that it is the Temple of Love, in which I am a living stone, the cornerstone of which is Christ; it is the Tree of Eternal Life, of which I am a branch; it is the Body of Christ on earth since His Ascension into Heaven and I am one of the cells of that Body."

The Body of Christ is therefore more to me than I am to myself; *Her* Life — I shall call the Body of Christ *her* because the Bible calls it His Spouse — Her life is more abundant than mine, for I live in union with Her, and without Her I have only a physical life. *Her* Loves are *my* loves; *Her* Truths are *my* truths; *Her* Mind is my mind. I consider that the greatest blessing Almighty God has given to me is to be united with Her. My greatest pain is not to serve Her better. Without Her I am the uprooted stem, an isolated column among dead and forgotten ruins. With Her, I profess Eternity and am not afraid. From Her Tabernacles I draw the Bread of Life, from Her Episcopal Hands the oil that strengthens and blesses and consecrates; from Her sanctuary lamp the assurance that Christ has not left us orphans.

As a Mother, I lay my head between Her Hands; as a Spouse I find in Her the sweet tranquilities of love; as a Rock plunged into Eternity to Her I fly in the storm of blood that sweeps the earth in war and hate. Her will I love when all earthly loves are ended, and with a "passionless passion and wild tranquility." Through her Body I still hear Eternal Wisdom speak with infallible Truth; In Her Body, I hear Christ's Power and Authority and I obey and am free. From Her Body, I receive Christ's Life in the Eucharist and His forgiveness in the confessional. I thank You, O Christ, that I am a member of Your Body! I almost forgot to tell you the Bible tells us: "His Body is the Church." What a joy to be a Catholic!

THE HISTORY OF A WORD

ADDRESS DELIVERED ON JANUARY 22, 1950

*"And the rain fell and the floods came and
the wind blew and beat upon that house, but
it did not fall; it was founded on a Rock."*
(Matthew 7:25)

Friends:

Did you know that there were three men in
history whose names were changed by God? But you
do know *certainly* that a religion that started an hour
ago is worthless — because it is man-made. Even a
religion that started 1900 years ago is not necessarily Divine. Really a Divine religion ought to go back
to the first moment when God created man. Then
we would have God's idea of religion, not yours and
mine.

If you study the history of revealed religion
you discover two facts: 1. God extends His Mercies
to humanity through a community of His choosing;
2. Over this chosen body He Divinely appoints a
man as its head and His vicar.

In the very beginning of history God made the

first man Adam as the head of humanity. As a father's crimes disgrace his family, so in a greater way Adam's sin became our sin. But God in His Mercy promised a Redeemer born of a woman Who would crush the spirit of evil.

When sin multiplies on the face of the earth, God saves humanity in the Flood, not by providing each man with an individual life-saver. Rather, He selects a small community over which He Divinely appoints one man — Noah. Through this little social body God promises blessings to the world.

Later on, God chooses another man, Abram, to be the head of a new race or religious body and with him He enters into a new covenant. "All the communities of the earth shall find blessing in you" (Genesis 12:3). It was the first time in history that God ever changed the name of a man. The True and Almighty God changes his name from Abram to Abraham, which means "Father of many nations." Through him, not only his own people, but the Gentiles are to be blessed. It is serious to take away a man's name, but obviously God did it to remind Abraham that his relation to the God-approved community was not personal, that is, his by right, but functional, i.e., because of the role he fulfilled in it as God's vicar.

After the death of Abraham, the headship of the new spiritual organism passed on to the *Divinely chosen* Isaac. Next came Jacob who, one night just before the dawn, underwent a spiritual conflict "as fierce as the battling of men"; it was known as wrestling with an angel. As Abraham's faith revealed *God's* spiritual strength, Jacob's triumph revealed *man's* spiritual strength. For the second time in history God changes the name of a man. He gives new and added power to the spiritual corporation or body which is destined to enrich the world through the coming of its Savior, as God says to Jacob: "You shall no longer be called Jacob, but *Israel* shall be your name" (Genesis 35:10).

Later, Moses was *appointed* by God as the *head* of the new chosen body as God said: "I will make you *My* own people and I will be your God" (Exodus 6:7). "My own people." How the Egyptians must have accused the Jews of narrowness and intolerance for saying that God had *made* them the instrument through which His blessings would pass to all the world. But after all, since we are interested in God's ways, not man's, so be it. Evidently God has not given to each an individual planet; there is only one sun to light a world.

After Moses, there is Joshua, and later David, and the Kings, and the Prophets. God never communicated His blessings to an individual for *himself alone, nor* to the *world* in general. He did it always through a *corporate* body with whom He entered into a *covenant* and over which *He chose* a head. Faithful or unfaithful, virtuous or sinful, infallible was the destiny of this Religious Body. God was to be with this instrument He had chosen. No matter what it did, even though it fell among idolators, even though some of the appointed heads were sinful, even though their love of the flesh damaged their efficiency, God's purposes went on and prevailed, for as it has been said: "God alone can write straight with crooked lines."

You can readily see that the most important word in the Old Testament was the word for this religious body of chosen people with its Divinely appointed head, through which God would come to redeem man from sin. The Hebrew word for this elect body, or the Divinely chosen community, was *Qahal*.

About two hundred years before Christ was born, so many Jews were scattered throughout a Grecian civilization that it became necessary to translate the Hebrew scriptures into Greek. This translation has since been called the *Septuagint*, because it was said to be done by seventy men. When they came across the word *Qahal*, which stood for the community which was *visible* in its members, and yet *invisible* in the Spirit of God that watched and protected it, these learned old men translated this important Hebrew word *Qahal*, which appears ninety-six times in the Old Testament, into the Greek word *Ecclesia*. (It will never hurt us to know a little Hebrew and Greek, so keep in mind these words *Qahal* [Hebrew] and *Ecclesia* [Greek], for they mean the same.)

Finally, in the fulness of time, He Whom the prophet foretold would be born in Bethlehem, and Who would be conceived by a Virgin, now appears as God in the form of man: Our Lord and Savior, Jesus Christ. He is born in the *Qahal* or *Ecclesia* of the Jewish people. That is what the Gospel means when it tells us He came "into His own." *But,* and this is important, He also said that He came not to *destroy* His *Qahal* or *Ecclesia,* but to *fulfill* it and *perfect it.* But before He would do this men would have to know Who He is, for He hit history with such an impact He split it in two.

The scene took place in the half-pagan city of Caesarea Philippi. He, the Lord and Master of the world, stopped to ask a question — the most important one He ever asked in His Life:

"What do *men* say of the Son of Man? Who do they think He is?" (Matthew 16:13). Notice: "What do *men* say?" It was a test for religion based on the majority idea, the poll, public opinion, or the individual's interpretation of his own emotional experiences. "What do *men* say?" The answer was one of total confusion. "Some say John the Baptist," they told Him, "others Elijah, others again Jeremiah, or one of the prophets" (Matthew 16:14). All rudimentary guesses of the poor and ignorant! No certainty! No agreement! No unity so dear to the Heart of God!

Leave the secret of His Divinity to polls, to masses and majority votes, and you get only contradictory, contrary, and confusing responses, one man denying what another has said! Our Lord had for this confusion only the withering scorn of His silence.

Our Lord now turns from quantity to quality, from the mob to the intelligentsia. He questions the Senate, the Federation, the Parliament, the House of Lords, as He says to them: "And *what* of you? Who do *you* say that I am?" (Matthew 16:15). *You,* My council, My followers! Not *men,* but "you." And the Twelve Apostles do not answer. Why are they silent? Because, perhaps, if they all spoke at once there would be only confusion of tongues; because, if one spoke for the others too, they would have asked who gave him authority to speak; because they knew down deep in their hearts that if the answer was to be based on the majority, then God's Truth would not be absolute.

There was no certitude in the conciliar body any more than among the individuals. Men will never agree among themselves; the best they can do is to federate their guesses. Such federation of opinions are like spiritual archipelagoes, little islands separated from one another by whirling waters of scepticism, and united only in fiction by a common name. There is no one to speak for them; there is no authority; there is *no head*; there is therefore no unity. A body without a head is a monstrosity whether the body be physical, social or religious.

Something now happens which is less of man than of God. One man now steps forward. It is he who is always mentioned first in every list of the Apostles.

He is named one hundred and ninety-five times in the Gospels, while all the other Apostles together are mentioned only one hundred and thirty times. He is the only person, outside of His Heavenly Father, whom Our Lord so united to Himself as to say: "We." He is also the third man in history whose name is changed by God. We may suspect then that as with Abraham and in Jacob, some new and unheard of perfection is to be given to the *Qahal* or *Ecclesia*. This man's original name was Simon, son of Jonah. When Our Lord first saw him, a year and a half before this scene, He said: "You are Simon, the son of Jonah"; then Our Lord changed his name: "You shall be called Cephas (which means rock)." He changes his name from Simon to Rock. We do not have the full flavor of this in English because Peter, the name of a man, is different from the word Rock. But in the original Aramaic, which Our Lord spoke, Cephas which is his new name means Rock. It is something like the French where the word *Pierre* means not only the name of a man, but also *rock*.

This same man whose name was changed to Rock now steps forward, not because the Apostles asked him to do so, not because he was smarter than the others, or because he knew the answer in his own flesh and blood, but because there came to him a great light, a light that made him first for eternity — That heavenly revelation gave him the answer to the question of the Master as with infallible certitude he affirms: "You are the Christ, the Son of the Living God" (Matthew 16:17).

Peter knew Who He was. He was not John the Baptist! He was not Elijah! *He was* the One to Whom the Gentile and Jewish world had been expectantly looking for so many centuries. He is Emmanuel! God with us! The Son of the Living God! Jesus Christ, True God and True Man! The *moment* he said it *he* was *certain* he had *Divine* assistance. And Our Lord told him that was *how* he knew it as He said: *"Blessed are you,* Simon, son of Jonah; for *flesh and blood* has not revealed this to you, but *My Father in Heaven"* (Matthew 16:18).

At this moment Simon, the descendant of Abraham who revealed the Power of *God,* and the descendant of Jacob who revealed the power of *man, combines* in himself the powerful initiative of a human will cooperating with the infallible assistance of a Heavenly Father. The God-Man who changed his name now sets him at the head of the new and perfected religious body, a new Israel, a new *Christ-Qahal,* a *Divine-Ecclesia* with these words: "And so I say to you, you are Peter, and upon this rock I will build my *Ecclesia* (I am not yet translating into English this Greek word used in the Gospels) and the gates of hell shall not prevail against it. I will give to *you* the keys to the Kingdom of Heaven; whatever you shall bind on earth shall be bound in Heaven, and whatever you shall loose on earth shall be loosed in Heaven" (Matthew 16:17-19).

Our Divine Lord leaves nothing undetermined about His new *Qahal* or *Ecclesia,* for He spoke of three things: its foundation, what is outside it, and what is inside it, and all three revolved about one man. The *foundation* is the Rock who is Peter; the door to the *Ecclesia* from the *outside* is to be opened by keys, and these keys swing from the cincture of Peter; once on the *inside* the same rock and key-bearer has the power to bind and loose, to seal and unseal consciences even for registry in the Book of Life.

Now the time has come to translate the word *Qahal* or *Ecclesia* into English. This past Summer while in Rome, my first visit was to the tomb of St. Peter. After reciting the Creed at the tomb of the Fisherman who made Rome eternal, I arose and took about two hundred and sixty-one steps and found myself kneeling before a man whose name was changed; it was Pacelli once, but is now Pius XII.

Those two hundred and sixty-one steps were like two hundred and sixty-one links in a chain of history binding Pius XII to Peter, Peter to Christ,

Christ to the *Qahal*, and, spiritual Semite that I am, binding me to Melchizedek, Abraham and Jacob and the *Qahal* of Israel.

As I entered into the happiness of an audience with him who is my spiritual father, I was conscious not only of my own personal unworthiness to be a member of Christ's Mystical Body, but also of my failure to spread more the knowledge and love of Our Lord. But at that moment when I knelt before him who is Cephas, Christ's Vicar, Chief Shepherd of the new *Qahal*, all my fears and sense of weakness vanished. I never knew there was so much love and fire in my heart for Christ's *Ecclesia* as there was at that moment when I saw the *Ecclesia* personalized in him. Later, I reflected: maybe that is the way we, who try to love God but fail occasionally, will be before the Judgment Seat of God. The sense of our failures will vanish. We will be utterly amazed at how much we really love God. From now on I shall never believe Judgment is hard, if we try to love Our Lord.

At the close of the audience, the Holy Father with burning accents of affection used that same word Our Lord used to his predecessor Peter, as he observed that the evil can be overcome only by the love for Christ in His Mystical Body, the *Ecclesia*. When I went back to the tomb of the Rock, I looked up to the greatest dome ever thrown against the vault of Heaven's blue, and Lo! There was the same word: *Ecclesia* — written across that dome in letters of gold, *"Tu es Petrus, et supra hanc petram aedificabo ecclesiam Meam."* Now I will translate those words of Our Lord: "You are Peter, and upon this rock I will build My Church" (Matthew 16:18).

Qahal, Ecclesia — *Ecclesiam Meam.* And the Church that the God-Man and Savior founded on a Rock, Our Lord calls *My Church.* Now you know why we Catholics love it. Wouldn't you?

God love you!

SCANDALS

ADDRESS DELIVERED ON JANUARY 29, 1950

"And blessed is the one who is not scandalized by Me." (Matthew 11:6)

Friends:

Every now and then people come across a counterfeit bill, but I never knew anyone who, because of it, argued that the United States currency was worthless. Astronomers have seen spots on the sun, but I have yet to hear of one who denied that the sun is the light of the world. But I know many who pick out the failings and sins of a few Catholics and then say: "But, my dear, they don't tell you everything! The Church is really the work of the Devil!"

This extreme point of view, starts with a fact: There are scandals! For example, some Catholic husbands and wives are unfaithful; some Catholic politicians are more crooked than those who have no religion; some Catholic boys steal; some Catholic girls worship the same saints as pagan girls: movie heroes or band leaders; some Catholic industrialists are selfish and hardhearted and totally indifferent to the rights of the workers; some Catholic labor leaders are more interested in keeping their leadership by annual strikes than in cooperating for social justice. Then in the Papacy, there is Alexander VI.

What does all this prove, but that Our Dear Lord has espoused humanity as it is, rather than as we would like it to be! He never expected His Mystical Body the Church to be without scandals because He Himself was the first scandal. It was a terrible scandal for those who knew Him to be God to see Him crucified and go down to seeming defeat, at the moment His enemies challenged Him to prove His Divinity by coming down from the Cross. No wonder He had to beg His followers not to be scandalized by Him. If the human nature of Our Lord could suffer physical defeat and be a scandal, why should there not be scandals in Our Lord's Mystical Body made up of poor mortals such as we? If He permitted thirst, pain and a death sentence to affect His Physical Body, why should He not permit mystical and moral weaknesses such as loss of faith, sin, scandals, heresies, schisms, and sacrileges to affect His Mystical Body? When these things do happen, it does not prove that the Mystical Body the Church is not Divine in its inmost nature, any more than the Crucifixion of Our Lord proved that He is not Divine. Because our hands are dirty, the whole body is not polluted. The scandals of the Mystical Body the Church no more destroy its *substantial* holiness than the Crucifixion destroyed the substantial wholeness of Christ's Physical Body. The Old Testament prophecy fulfilled on Calvary was that not a bone of His Body would be broken. His flesh would hang like purple rags about Him, wounds like poor dumb mouths would speak their pain with blood, pierced hands and feet would open up torrents of redemptive life — but His *substance,* his bones, they would be sound. So with His Mystical Body. Not a bone of it shall ever be broken; the substance of Her Doctrines will always be pure, though the flesh of some of Her doctors fail; the substance of Her Discipline will always be sound, though the passions of some of her disciples rebel; the substance of Her Faith will always be Divine though the flesh of some of her faithful will be so carnal. Her Wounds will never be mortal, for Her Soul is Holy and Immortal, with the Immortality of Love Divine that came to Her Body on the Day of Pentecost as tongues of living fire.

Coming to one of the major scandals, let it be asked: "How could a wicked man like Alexander VI be the infallible Vicar of Christ and head of His Mystical Body the Church?" For an answer, go to the Gospel text where Our Lord changes the name of Simon to Rock, and then made him the Rock on which He built what He called "My Church." Our Lord on that very occasion made a distinction very few ever think of: He distinguished between infallibility or immunity from error, and impeccability or immunity from sin. Infallibility is inability to *teach* what is wrong; impeccability is inability to *do* wrong. Our Lord made the Rock infallible, but not impeccable.

Immediately after assuring Peter that he had the keys of Heaven and authority to bind and loose, Our Blessed Lord tells His Apostles that He "must go up to Jerusalem," and "must be put to death" (Matthew 16:21.) Poor, weak, human Peter, proud of his authority as the Rock draws Our Lord to his side, and begins rebuking Him, saying: "God forbid, Lord! No such thing shall ever happen to You" (Matthew 16:22). On hearing these words Our Lord "turned around and said to Peter. 'Get behind Me, Satan! You are an obstacle to Me. You are thinking not as God does, but as human beings do'" (Matthew 16:23).

A moment before Peter was called the Rock; now he is called Satan! In so many words Our Lord was telling him: "As the Rock upon which I build My Church, whenever you speak with the assistance of Heaven, you shall be preserved from error; but as Simon, son of Jonah, as a *man*, you are so frail, so carnal, so apt to be sinful, that you can become even like unto Satan. In your office you, as Peter, are infallible; but as a man, Simon, you are peccable. The Power you have as Peter is My Making; the want of morals you have as Simon, is of your making." Is this distinction between a person and his function hard to grasp? If a policeman directing traffic held up his hand and ordered you to stop, you would do so, even though you knew he beat his wife. And why? Because you make a distinction between his function as a representative of law and his person. I am sure that Our Lord permitted the fall of Peter immediately after the gift of Primacy to remind him and all his successors that infallibility would belong necessarily to his office, but virtue would have to be acquired by his own striving with the help of God's grace. Whether the voice be sweet, or dull and grating, whether it be spoken with an accent or a flaw in grammar, we consider not the tone but the message. "Speak, Lord, for Your servant is listening" (1 Samuel 3:9).

It is generally safe to say that those who know everything about the few bad successors of Peter, know nothing at all about the very many good ones. The wickedness of one man in authority is allowed to obscure a million saints. How many who dwell on the Vicars of Christ during the brief period of the Renaissance, ever dwell on their history for the other 1900 years? How many of those who exploit the bad few ever admit that of the first thirty-three successors of Peter, thirty were martyrs for their Faith, and the other three exiled for it? How many of those who concentrate on the bad example of a few know, or ever admit, that of the two hundred and sixty-one successors of St. Peter, eighty-three have been canonized for their heroic virtue, and that over fifty were chosen over the protest of their own unworthiness for such a high office, and that few can match in humility, wisdom and learning our present Holy Father, Pius XII? Anyone who attacks such a long line of martyrs, saints, and scholars must be certain of his own *sinlessness* to lay his hand on the few who revealed the human side of their office. If the revilers themselves are holy, pure and undefiled, let them pick up their stones. Our Lord said that it is the privilege only of those who are without sin to cast the first stone. But if they are *not* without sin, then let them leave the judgment to God. If they are without sin, they belong to a different race from you and me, for from down deep in our hearts a cry comes to our lips: "Be merciful to me a sinner."

Turning to the scandal of bad Catholics, it must be remembered that Our Lord no more expected to have every member of His Church perfect than He expected to have perfect Apostles. That is why He said that on the last day He would throw the bad fish out of His net. Some Catholics may be bad, but that does not prove the Mystical Body is wicked, any more than because a few Americans who sell themselves to Russia, proves that America is a race of traitors. Our Faith increases responsibility, but it does not force obedience; it increases blame but it does not prevent sin. If some Catholics are bad, it is not because they are members of Christ's Mystical Body, but rather because they are not living up to its Lights and Grace.

The psychology of those who are scandalized at bad Catholics is interesting. It means that they expected something better; if people who themselves are wicked, rejoice in the scandal, it is because they think they have greater authority for sinning than anyone else who fell. One never hears it said: "He is a bad Relativist," or he is a "scandalous Humanist" or an "adulterous Ethicist," because they never really expected anything better from them in the beginning. The horror that one feels at those who fall, is the measure of the height of virtue to which they expected them to stand. We are grateful for the compliment of their being scandalized at our weak members, and for being intolerant with us about the very things they tolerate in others. They know that there are no other new lights possible if the sun fails! It is intellectually stultifying and morally easy to be a Communist; it is intellectually refreshing and morally hard to be a Catholic.

No ideal is more difficult of attainment. When anyone falls away from a Sun Cult he never has very far to tumble. But when a Catholic falls away, he is apt to be far worse than anyone else. The greater the height from which he falls, the greater the splash. "The corruption of the best is the worst." No flowers smell worse than the rotted lily.

May we ask those who are scandalized with the failings of the Church, how perfect the Church would have to be before they would become incorporated into it as a living cell? If it were as perfect as they wanted it to be, do they realize that there would be no room for them? Just suppose for a moment, that Christ's Mystical Body had no moral weaknesses; suppose that no monk ever broke his priestly vows to marry a nun and start a new religion — and this really happened; suppose that no bishop was ever just a business administrator, and no priest ever disedifying, and no monk ever fat, and no sister ever cross to children, and sanctity was as automatic as a parking meter; and suppose no one ever gave scandal to those who are on the outside to justify the way they were living. Would such a Church be the kind that Our Lord envisaged Who told us that cockle would be sowed with wheat, and that some of the children of the Kingdom would be cast out? If the Mystical Body were as perfect as the scandalized would have it, would not Her very perfection accuse and condemn us who are not saintly? Too high an ideal often *repels* rather than attracts. She would be so saintly that she would no longer allure ordinary mortals. She might even appear to the struggling souls as terribly Puritan, easily scandalized at our failings, and might even shrink from having Her garments touched by sinners like ourselves. Gone then would be the hope for those who are unholy or in sin. No! The Mystical Body with none but perfect members would be a stumbling block. Then, instead of us being scandalized by Her, She would be scandalized by us, which would be far worse.

If the life of the Mystical Body had been one triumphant, blazing transfiguration on a mountain top, apart from the woes and ills of man, She would never have been the comforter of the afflicted and the refuge of sinners. She has been called like Her Divine Head, to be a redemptress, lifting men from the shadows of sin to be the tabernacles of grace where saints are made. She is not a far-off, abstract idea, but a Mother, and though She has been stained with dust in Her long journey through the centuries, and though some of Her children have nailed Her Body and saddened Her Soul, yet there is joy in Her Heart because of the children She has nourished; there is gladness in Her eyes, because of the faith She has preserved; there is understanding in Her soul, for She has understood the frailty of our flesh, and knows how to nourish it back to life. And in these qualities one divines the reason why Our Lord chose, not a saintly man like John, but a weak, fallen man like Peter as His First Vicar, in order that through his weakness he, and the Church of which he is the head, might sympathize with the weakness of his brethren, be their apostle of mercy and, in the truest sense of the term, the vicar of the Savior and

Redeemer of the world, Who came not to save the just but me, a sinner.

Our Lord often punishes His Mystical Body from time to time, by permitting some of the members or cells of that Body to separate themselves from it, but He punishes them still more. On the whole the world is right! We Catholics are not all we ought to be! The world is the way it is, because we Catholics are the way we are. Our Lord said: "If salt loses its taste, what is there left to give taste to it?" (Matthew 5:13) It is not the world we have failed, but Christ, and in failing Christ, we failed the world. But we beg those of you who see our failings to remember how hard it is for us to be everything Our Lord wants us to be. It is so easy to be a Democrat or a Republican or a "Cosmic Unifier," but it is very hard to be a Catholic! Judge us not by our failings, as you judge not art by the feeble scribblings of a child. Look rather to our artistic masterpieces: the saints, and there are countless armies of them in the world. We have hurt you by our failings, and we beg your pardon, but we hurt Our Dear Lord more, and we shall do penance.

There are many of you who are scandalized by us, who, if you had the same Infallible Truth to guide you, the same Divine Eucharist to nourish you daily, would be a thousand times better than we are. We ought to be better than we are. And here I touch on the only unhappiness that comes to us as Catholics, and believe me, it is very real! We are unhappy because we are not saints. Will you therefore pray for us? Thanks!

God love you!

OUR LORD'S MEMORIAL DAY

ADDRESS DELIVERED ON FEBRUARY 5, 1950

"Do this in memory of Me." (Luke 22:19)

Friends:

One of the truly beautiful traits of the American people is the way they honor their soldier dead on Memorial Day. What village is there without its scroll, what city without its monument, and what patriotic heart is unmindful of their sacrifice? Every Memorial unites the three tenses of time: the past, the present and the future. In the *present* is the celebration honoring our heroes; the *past* is recalled in recounting the battles they fought and the sacrifices they made; the *future* as we pledge ourselves to keep the freedom they won.

But all their sacrifices were inspired by Him Who offered His Life for our Redemption in the Battle of Calvary. This Soldier-Christ is the only one Who ever came into this world to die; everyone else came into it to live. Death was a stumbling block to *other* heroes; it interrupted their mission. But it was the goal of His Life, the gold He was seeking. But unlike soldiers who have to trust to our goodness to recall their death, Our Lord took no such chances with the short memories of men. He Himself instituted the precise Memorial by which His Death would be recalled and applied. The night before He died, He made His Last Will and Testament, and left something which no dying man before or since was ever able to leave: His Very Self in the Memorial of His Death. At the Last Supper He instituted not a Memorial Day but a Memorial Act and then told His Church: "Do this in memory of Me," that is, repeat it, recall My Death! have a Memorial Day from the rising to the setting of the sun!

There is a right and wrong way of looking on His Death, as a drama may be considered from two distinct points of view. In one instance, suppose a great drama was produced only once and in only one city of the world. After that unique production, if you wanted to know about it, you would read a review of it written by four drama critics, who would tell you the characters who acted in it, quote a line here and there, and give you snatches of the plot to create an emotional glow. Now consider the drama from another point of view. Suppose that the drama after it played on the opening night, was given to road companies to perform, and that following the injunctions of the author they travelled all over the world with the script, giving many people who had a talent for it, an opportunity of acting in that drama.

The first point of view corresponds to those who think that the Death of Our Lord on Calvary is something that happened once, like the death of Socrates, and that our only contact with it is to read what the four Gospels have to say about it. The second point of view corresponds to the wishes of Our Divine Lord — Calvary is a continuing Act in a great Eternal Drama. Its *script* was written in Heaven when the world was created, for Sacred Scripture tells us that Our Lord is "the Lamb slain from the beginning of the world." The moment freedom was given to men the crucifixion was possible. Then came the rehearsals for this Tragedy all through the Old Testament, in Abraham, and Isaac, the brazen serpent and the Paschal Lamb. Then the curtain went up on the Opening Night which was called Good Friday, when the Great Tragedian, Christ, offered His Life for the sins of the world, in accordance with the script that had been written by His Heavenly Father. Immediately afterwards, in accordance with His instructions, the Tragedy of Calvary is repeated throughout the world, thanks to the road companies which are playing to packed houses every day even to this very hour. This re-presentation and re-enactment of the Sacrifice of Christ on the Cross, applied to our day and to our lives, is the Mass. In the Mass, the Mystical Body of Christ actually united to Christ, its Head, offers through Him and with Him the Sacrifice of Calvary.

This Memorial of His Death, like Memorial Day, has the same three tenses: in the *present* we recall the *past* for the sake of the *future*.

The past. How beautifully and mysteriously the Death of Our Lord is recalled and prolonged in the Mass. Our Lord died on the Cross by the separation of His Blood from His Body. In anticipation of His Death the next day, Our Lord at the Last Supper did not change the bread and wine together into His Body and Blood. First He changed the bread into His Body; then the wine into His Blood. In the Consecration of the Mass, following His orders, we do the same. This separate consecration of the bread and wine is like a mystical sword separating His Body from His Blood, which is the way He died on the Cross. Thus instead of a stone tribute to a dead hero, we have the Same Sacrifice, and the Same Priest, as was offered on Calvary.

The present. But this Memorial of His Death He asked to be repeated, so we reenact it in the present. On the Cross we were potentially united to Christ as the Head of the Mystical Body; but in the Mass we actualize that union. On the Cross, Our Lord in a certain sense was alone. But in the Mass, we, the members of the Mystical Body, are with Him. For example, it is one thing to have a health program sent out from a broadcasting station; it is quite another thing to tune in that program and apply those health directives to oneself. It is one thing for Christ to redeem us; it is quite another thing to apply that Redemption. Through the Consecration, Christ becomes present on the altar with all those sentiments which He had on the Cross. But something is added: we sacrifice ourselves or make ourselves die to sin with Him. In every Mass we picture Our Lord looking out from Heaven, saying to us: "This human nature which I took from Mary, and which I offered as a Spotless sacrifice for you, is now glorified at the right Hand of My Father. I cannot die in it again. But I can prolong My Redemption, make it living, vital, and personal to you, if you will give Me by a free act of your will, *your* human nature. Then I can die in you, and you can die in Me. Then the Cross will not be something which happened, but which is happening. Remember I said you must take up your cross daily. This is where you take it up, to die with Me and in Me. So Peter and Paul, Mary and Anne, James and John, William and Joseph, will you give Me your human nature, as Mary gave me mine? Your sacrifices whatever they be, are vain unless they are offered in and through Me, the One Priest the One Victim. Since I died to sin in My human nature and rose to newness of Life and Glory, I want you to actualize and apply that death to yourself, by *dying* to your sins, and thus prepare for your newness of life and eternal glory.

"Will you therefore at the moment of this Memorial say to Me: 'My Jesus, this is *my* body, this is *my* blood. Take it, change it, consecrate it, crucify it, make it die with Thee, that all that is evil in me may perish on the Cross and that all that is good in me may live on only in You. I care not if the species of my life remain, the mere appearances of bread and wine, the duties of my daily routine or my physical appearance. Let these remain before the eyes of men. But all that I am, divinize, change, transubstantiate, so that the Heavenly Father looking down may not see me, but Thee, or rather me hidden in Thee, dead to the world of sin, and say: "You are My beloved Son in whom I am well pleased."'"

But there is also the *future*. On Memorial Day we pledge to keep faith with the dead that the freedom they won for us will remain our heritage. In this Memorial of Calvary, there is not a verbal but a vital pouring out of the Christ-Life into the members of His Mystical Body, guaranteeing the future in two ways, not only our personal immortality, but also the continued Divine Preservation of the Mystical Body against the gates of hell, until the consummation of the world. It has always been a mystery to the carnal-minded how the Mystical Body the Church has continued as a living unit in faith and morals under the authority of Peter ever since the days of Our Lord. They try to account for it by its organization. But this is not the answer. The secret of Catholic Power is communion with the Divine. You cannot put your finger on the secret of its growth and strength. As Our Lord said: "The coming of the Kingdom of God cannot be observed by human eyes" (Luke 17:20). It is like a small willow tree weighing five pounds which a pre-Bolshevik Russian scientist planted in a box which contained two hundred pounds of soil. After five years, the willow tree was taken out, and every grain of soil was carefully removed. The tree now weighed 169 pounds. But the soil lost only two ounces. Where did the 164 pounds of increase come from? Not from anything material. The answer is that all the while the tree was in communion with the great invisible forces of the air and sunlight. In like manner, the growth and increase of Christ's Mystical Body through the ages is not due to its organization or administration, for God knows that it is not always the highest and the best. Rather its unity and power and growth come from the Divine Christ Whose Body and Blood, Soul and Divinity we receive in Holy Communion, which unites us not only to Him, but also to one another as members of His Mystical Body.

Your physical body is made up of millions and millions of cells; and these cells need nourishment which is supplied by blood plasma or lymph. It courses through all the gates and alleys of the body to nourish and repair. It knocks at the door of each individual cell, offers all its treasures and bids the customers tap it for what is needed. Though each cell retains its distinctive individuality, yet all are bathed and unified in the corporate contribution.

This nourishing blood plasma in the human body is a faint, far-off echo of what Our Lord has provided for His Mystical Body. Instead of cells, there are persons; instead of human nourishment, there is the Divine Bread of Life, the Eucharist. The life of the body is the soul; the life of the soul is Christ. As the body-life receives its communion with lymph, so the Mystical Body receives its communion with the Christ in the Eucharist. This Divine Blood Plasma, which sustains each person in his spiritual life, is the same which every other person in the Mystical Body receives. This is the basic reason why the Mystical Body the Church is one. "Because the loaf of bread is one, we, though many, are one body, for we all partake of the one loaf" (1 Corinthians 10:17). The Communion Rail is, therefore, the most democratic institution in the history of the world. Everyone who receives the Body and Blood of Christ has the same Divine Life flowing through his veins as flows through mine. The Christ-life in me, is the same Christ-life in all other members of the Mystical Body; therefore, each of them is my brother and my sister in Christ. Communion is for the Community! Such is the beautiful fellowship of our Faith!

Because the Christ-life is the Divine Plasma of

the Mystical Body its future is necessarily immortal; those who look for the destruction of the Church in the future should better look for the daily drowning of the morning star. Our Lord was not fooling when He told Peter: "The gates of hell shall not prevail against My Church."

What would the world do without the Mass? Suffering used to be the lot of a few. Today it is the burden of everybody. If it is not bodies who are in pain, it is minds with their anxieties, fears and worries. Oh, the tragedy of all this wasted pain! It is almost unbearable for many because so few have anyone to love. Love cannot destroy pain, but it can lessen it, just as you mind less the loss of your purse if a starving family was fed through finding it. So our sorrows can become light when we offer them up for someone we love. If each morning we would take all our little crosses to Mass, and plant them alongside Our Lord's Great Cross on Calvary, and then at the moment of Consecration say with Him: "This is *my* body, this is *my* blood," we would forget we had any sufferings — so ecstatic would be our Love of Jesus Crucified!

That my words may be a deed of love, tomorrow morning I shall offer the Holy Sacrifice of the Mass for all who hear this broadcast. May you Catholics actively share in it by attending Mass tomorrow in your parish Church. Thanks!

God love you!

HOW IT FEELS TO BE
A CATHOLIC

ADDRESS DELIVERED ON FEBRUARY 12, 1950

*"In the world, you will find tribulation; but
take courage, I have conquered the world."*
(John 16:33)

Friends:

If we wanted to know about mining, we would never
go to a man who was never down in a mine. But in
the field of religion, he who never prays is often
accepted as an authority on the Church. The time
has come for someone inside Christ's Mystical Body
to tell you how it feels to be a Catholic.

In a single line it can be described in a para-
dox: A Catholic is one who experiences at one and
the same moment a seeming contradiction: an inquietude and a peace. First the inquietude. Obviously, it is not the false restlessness of those who
have not yet found God, or who, having found Him,
lost Him through sin. Our inquietude has a double
source: (1) The sublimity of the Ideal; (2) The tension of body and soul.

First, our inquietude comes from a realization of our failings in the face of Infinite Love. It is so easy to be a liberal in politics, but it is very difficult to be liberal with God. The world is full of tiny little egos who imitate God the Creator and make of themselves little tin gods; but how few there are who want to be like their Crucified Savior. It cost so much to tame our lower nature and thus fulfill the words of Paul: "Those who belong to Christ have crucified their flesh with all its passions and desires" (Galatians 5:24). We have a temptation to pull back, lest His wounded Hands touch ours and leave an imprint: We look up to the altar during Mass and see not a cross which is a contradiction, but a crucifix which is a summons to the Great Captain bearing Five Scars in the forefront of battle; then we glance down at our lily white hands and are scandalized that we have come down from Calvary with hands unscarred and white. Even when we do try our best, when we serve our neighbor as if he were Christ, and welcome the stranger into our home as if he were the Lord Himself, we are tempted to think we have done well. But lo! There comes to our minds the reminder of Our Lord that when we have done everything well, we are but to consider ourselves as "unprofitable servants." It is a psychological fact that the more we try to serve Our Lord's Mystical Body the greater becomes our feeling of dissatisfaction; the closer we get to Him, the more we become convinced that we are doing nothing. This is due to the infinity of our ideals. A painting in candle light may seem artistic, but as soon as it is brought into the sunlight, it turns out to be a daub. So when we judge ourselves by worldly standards, we are pleased with ourselves; but as soon as we bring ourselves into the Light of Christ, we shrink in horror at what we see, and say with Peter: "Depart from me, O Lord, for I am a sinful man" (Luke 5:9). The farther we depart from the Divine Ideal, the more we boast of our perfections; but the closer we get to Him, the more we see our imperfections. This is our pain. No one feels assured of his innocence in the face of Absolute Purity, but asks with the Apostles at the Last Supper: "Is it I Lord? Is it I?" (Matthew 26:22).

The inquietude and restlessness has a second origin in the terrific tension between body and soul, or better, the inadequacy of the body to follow the soul. Like caged birds there come moments of great aspiration to be with God, particularly after Communion, and yet our body weighs us down, cabins, cribs and confines our soul. The best of romantic poetry is a cry and a moan. In the face of earthly beauty the heart suffers from its own inadequacy. If earthly lovers feel powerless to express their love for a human, then what shall the human soul feel in the face of "that Love we fall just short of in all love." There is never any love between equals. But there is justice. The so-called equality of the sexes is fatal to love. In love there is an overwhelming sense not of equality, but of the inferiority of the lover and the superiority of the beloved. The lover must always be on his knees, the beloved on a pedestal. Every lover grieves over his unworthiness. Lift this psychological experiment to the Infinite at the moment of greatest intimacy when we receive in Communion the Lord of Love and Life. Is it any wonder the Church puts on our lips at that moment these words: "Lord, I am not worthy that You should enter under my roof." Nothing we can say to the Divine Visitor of our soul seems to convey our love. Along with our insatiable passion to love more, there is a depressing sense of our adolescence in the face of the Eternal. We know we are offering weeds when we ought to give roses; we have a feeling of being burnt out cinders when we ought to be living coals of fire; of having arms that do not close tightly on the Spirit, when we ought to have wings to nest with the Eternal. On top of all this, there is the terrible feeling of *not* loving enough, of being empty, cold, distracted with the Beloved, when nothing can satisfy except being owned and wooed by Him as the branches to the Vine. The deeper our faith, the keener our impatience to see the fulness of Light; the keener the hope, the more passionate our desire to be possessed; the warmer the love, the more we pull at the veils of flesh which must be worn, and yet hide the Beauty of that Face that "leaves all other beauty pain."

In brief, ours is the inquietude of the lover who as yet is separated from the beloved; ours is the anxiety which St. Augustine described: "Our hearts were made for Thee, O God, and they are restless until they rest in Thee."

But this is only one side of the picture. Alongside of this pain which comes from our unworthiness there is an ineffable peace and an indescribable joy. First, there is the intellectual joy of knowing the Truth of Christ, prolonged through His Mystical Body, the Church. I can convey an idea of this peace to those of you who believe in the Divinity of Christ. Suppose you lived in the days of Our Lord, and you wanted to know the attitude of the Son of God to a totalitarian government which was absorbing and swallowing up all Asia Minor. One day you heard Christ tell the Commissar Pilate: "You would have no power unless it were given to you from above." You would have accepted those words as the infallible Truth of the Son of God on the subject of political power, even though He spoke them only through a human nature. We no more doubt the Infallibility of Christ's Truth when He spoke through a human Body to Commissar Pilate, than we doubt His Infallibility when He speaks through His Mystical Body to a Commissar Stalin. As my invisible mind communicates a truth, in this broadcast through my visible head and body, so the invisible Head of the Mystical Body, Christ, communicates His Truth today through His visible Head, Peter, and His Mystical Body. For example, when I point to two apples and two apples and say they make four apples, is that truth any different than the spiritual, invisible truth I have in my mind that 2 plus 2 equals four? All that I do is to apply an eternal spiritual truth to new historical and concrete circumstances; but it is no new truth.

So, when the Holy Father speaks as the visible Head of Christ's Mystical Body he does not create a new truth; he has not the power to do that; he does not speak in his own right, for in his person he is no more infallible than you or I, as your skull separated from your soul and body is worthless. *But* when he exercises his function as the Key Bearer and the Rock, he makes applicable to our times and articulates for our troubled conditions the Truth and the Mind of Christ.

It is a wonderful peace to have the Christ Mind as a guide in these troubled days. Let me give you an example. Long before the war, the Christ Mind of the Church condemned all three totalitarian systems, Nazism, Fascism and Communism as intrinsically wicked. During the war, when the Western World thought only two were evil, when no one was allowed to say anything against Communism, I once tried in a broadcast to bring out the fallacy of driving out the black and brown devils of Fascism and Nazism with the red devil of Communism. To overcome censorship, I disguised my idea of the Christ Mind that all three were wicked by quoting the words of Our Lord: "You cannot drive out the Devil with Beelzebub." But they would not allow me to say it. The Devil quoted Scripture against Our Lord but I found that the world will not allow Scripture to be quoted against the Devil. But who is there today who does not realize that the Infallible Christ Mind was right and the world was wrong, for Communism which in January 1945 enslaved only 190,000,000 people now enslaves 800,000,000. The only trouble with the Christ Mind or the infallibility of the Church is it is ahead of the times. The world is always reactionary.

The Christ Mind in the Encyclicals, also gives guidance on all phases of moral life, for example, whether it is lawful to murder sick people, even under the name of Euthanasia; whether the bombing of civilians is lawful; whether the capitalist's right to property is unlimited; whether the laborer's right to organize is independent of the common good; whether a world government shall be based on law or on power; whether the atomic bomb should be used. In this connection, here are the words of our Holy Father two years before the atomic bomb was known by the world, and two years before the first atomic bomb was dropped. This warning of the

Holy Father no newspaper in America printed. After giving the exact explosive power of the atomic bomb he warned: "The energy originated by atomic fission should not be used for bombs, but it should be controlled by suitable scientific means. Otherwise, a dangerous catastrophe could result, not only in a single place in the world, but even for our *entire planet.*" In other words, with our science divorced from morals, we could blow up the earth.

This is the Christ Mind on the subject of the atomic bomb! We thank God in His Mercy, not only for sending His Divine Son to teach Galilee and Judea in His physical Body, but also for teaching Washington, London and Moscow, Kickapoo and Rapid City in His Mystical Body. God destroyed sinful humanity once with water; will our godless, mad, leaderless world now destroy itself by fire? We know not, but it is possible! There really is only one security against the hydrogen bomb — keep in the state of grace.

There is not only peace for the intellect through the Truth of the Christ Mind, there is joy for the will, through the love of the Christ Heart. For example, in romantic love, the lover seeks to be pleasing to the beloved. A woman dresses in a certain color, wears her hair a certain way, all to make herself more attractive to the beloved and avoids all that would annoy or displease him. The true lover of Christ does not refrain from sin because he would break a commandment, but because he shrinks from hurting the beloved, Christ. Love has its necessities — to please, to obey, to be one in mind and heart with God regardless of what anyone says or does. To be in love with God changes our outlook on the world. We find that we love everyone in it, because they are made by Him and for Him; if the Divine Lover loves them, so do I.

This does not mean that we are immune from struggles and trials, but they are seen as coming from the Hands of the all-loving Father. All human systems and sentimental religions can stand up in the sunshine and prosperity, but in the face of death, disaster and catastrophe, they are as unsustaining as the breeze. In sorrow, our holy faith reminds us that we were born in tragedy — the defeat of Good Friday. The crucifix on the walls of our homes, the crucifix above our altar, the crucifix in our prayer books — all these tell us of the Divine Goodness Who took the worst that the world had to offer in the way of evil, and overcame it. We know Our Lord never told us we would be without trial, but He did tell us that we would never be overcome by it. That is why in grief, in suffering, in crisis, those who are sustained by the Christ-Love in the Mass, hardly ever go to pieces. Dr. Carl Jung, the world's celebrated non-Catholic psychiatrist, said that in thirty years of psychiatric practice he never found over four or five practicing Catholics who broke mentally under trial. There is joy in the soul of the faithful even when the body suffers; but there is never pain in the body that penetrates into the soul.

This is how it feels to be a Catholic; to be restless, to be at peace. These are not contradictions, for both our inquietude and our serenity are reconciled in love. We are restless because we do not possess Our Lord completely; we are serene to the extent that we do. The common fountain is love. Because we love the Infinite, we strain at the leash of the finite; because He touches our finger, we are in ecstacy knowing that one day He will take our hand. We are restless because we love so little; we are at peace because there is so much to love! We are envied for our peace and happiness; we are despised because its price is the Cross.

May I ask you this favor? The next time you hear a Communist agent say that America is a country of slaves, do not believe him. Ask a true American! The next time you want to find out how it feels to be at peace, do not ask those who spread lies about us; ask one of us who each morning at Mass receives into his heart in Communion the Christ Who is Our Truth, Our Peace and Our Joy.

God love you!

RUSSIA AND THE MYSTICAL BODY OF CHRIST

ADDRESS DELIVERED ON FEBRUARY 19, 1950

*"Love your enemies, do good to those who
hate you, pray for those who persecute and
insult you."* (Matthew 5:44, 45)

Friends:

For 33 years Communism has been trying to convince the world there is no God. But it has succeeded in convincing the world there is a Devil. The Mystical Body of Christ has probably had more martyrs for the faith in the last 33 years, than in 200 years of the Roman persecution. The diabolism of the present persecution is frightening. All hell broke loose in the living martyrdom of Cardinal Mindszenty. The Communist psychiatrist in charge of that ordeal had spent two years in Russia learning the brutality of Communist persecution. Through various tortures meant to kill the mind, this psychiatrist brought the Cardinal to the point of death. At that split second where the soul was about to leave the body, he boasted that Communist science could breathe a new soul into the Cardinal; i.e., take out the Christ-soul and put in the Soviet or Devil-soul. He hoped that he could create an entirely new personality in the Cardinal whom he would then bring before the people to denounce Christ and glorify the Soviets. This experiment, of course, failed because God, alone, can breathe a soul into a body. When the Cardinal answered the psychiatrist in Latin with the words of Our Lord, in desperation and frustration the psychiatrist screamed, "If Jesus could drive a devil out of a man, why cannot we put a devil into a man?"

Let me tell you the attitude of the Mystical Body, the Church, first, to Communism, and then to Russia. The Church makes a distinction between Russia and Communism. Russia is a country of human beings made to the image and likeness of God. Communism is an ideology which will vanish without destroying the Russian people. The Russian people are to be loved, even when they are Communists. But Communism as a system is to be rejected as intrinsically wicked.

The religious attitude of the Mystical Body of Christ toward Communism is quite different from the political attitude of the Western world. The Church judges Communism by its philosophy; the Western world judges it by its foreign policy. When the foreign policy of Communism is favorable to the Western world, the Western world accepts Communism as democratic; when the foreign policy of

Communism is inimical to the Western powers, they oppose Communism. This accounts for the changed attitude of the Western world to Communism in the last 25 years. At one time it regarded Communism as a great economic experiment in democracy; at another moment it sees it as a barbarian imperialistic force ready to destroy civilization. But no change in foreign policy altered the view of the Church.

Just as murder is wrong even though it is done under the name of Euthanasia, so, to the Church, Communism is wrong even when it kills in the name of democracy. But though it is evil, the Church knows that God can make evil serve goodness. Communism is like dung, first of all because it is the final decay of the materialism, agnosticism and atheism of 19th Century Europe; secondly, because it is a fertilizer. When Our Lord saw a barren fig tree, He said: "Dig and dung it." In His Wisdom, God may be permitting our Western world that has become barren from its Godlessness, to be fertilized with the dung of Communism. If its putrescence ever becomes the purging of our ways through violence, then God in His Mercy will change its nature like all fertilizers, and allow it to be taken up into the Tree of Life of a newer and better world.

The Russian people must be very confused at the changing mentality of the Western world. For twenty-five years the Western world allowed Communism to grow fat in its iron cage, even aiding its evil by sending its engineers and scientists and machinery to build up its world slavery. Now the Russian people through the Voice of America hear the very system, which once was praised, denounced as cruel and evil. They must suspect this sudden interest in their welfare, and ask themselves: "Is the Western world really interested in freeing us or is it trying to save its own skin?"

Suppose your next door neighbor supplied burglar tools to a thief to rob you. Then after having lost your property and having had your child murdered by the thief, the neighbor called you on the phone one day to tell you how vicious the robbers were, and that he was so interested in your welfare he wanted to give you a new electric can opener for the old one that you had in your kitchen. Would you not suspect *his* intentions? The Russian people must feel exactly the same way towards us. It must seem ironical to them that after twenty-five years of willful neglect when through the blood, sweat and tears they were sentenced to death by the millions, that now the Western world finds nothing better to offer their famished soul than the contents of a Sears and Roebuck catalogue. They must ask themselves: "Why should we give up a tyrannical materialism for a benign materialism when it is materialism we want to forget?"

This brings us to the attitude of the Church to Russia. If this broadcast ever penetrates beyond the Iron Curtain, and please God and Our Lady of Fatima it will, we want to tell the Russian people that as our brothers and sisters in Christ, they are closer to us than to the materialists of our Western world; And, yes, even more! That they have certain qualities which both we of Christ's Mystical Body and the Western world need for the betterment of the world. May God grant that some day we may incorporate into our lives their deep passions which revolve around that word which is the key to the Russian character: *Dousha* which means soul.

No other people on the face of the earth have such an acute sense of not being made for this world. Every Russian is a displaced person; an eternal up-rooted; a vagrant and a wanderer on the earth but conscious that he was once a King in the golden age of the Spirit. (In this he is a little like the Irish.) He has never forgotten the Fall and gropes and feels his way back to Heaven, even when he seems to be moving from it. Their own Lermontov has put it well in his famous poem *The Angel* in which the human soul can never forget the song sung by the angel who bore him to earth:

> "And long on this earth the soul tormented
>   itself
> Full of secret desire.
> But the dull songs of earth could not make it
>   forget
> The Songs it heard in heaven."

The most common word found on the lips of the Russian is the word *dousha*. When you come into their home they say: "My soul, will you sit down to tea?" In English we very often use the word *body*. For example, "I saw somebody on the street." In Russia they use the word *soul*, and instead of saying "Let me tell you something," they say: 'Let me unburden my soul to your soul." The term *dousha* becomes even a word of endearment in *doushinka* or else expresses a deep and profound yearning. When the Russian says: "There is nothing for the soul," he means, "There is no remedy for the situation." To have something for the soul, on the contrary, is to be synonymous with being at home.

The Russian soul is like their vast rolling lands, which is almost without limits; vain is he who tries to fill what they call the "broad Russian soul" with husks. So sensitive are they to the soul that they distinguish between sinning with the body and sinning with the soul. They believe that they can be foul in one and clean in the other. As a Russian woman told her lover after a quarrel: "You have my body, but my soul is mine." False though this be, there is behind it a deep sense of the eternal worth of an immortal soul. The Communists knew it, and at the beginning of the Revolution told the Russian people that they wanted to help their *dousha*. By a curious twist, the people have kept their *dousha* clean while their bodies are tormented.

No greater fury is aroused among their tormentors than to know that they can kill the Russian body and yet not touch the Russian soul. The Russians know they cannot do that, for even in Siberia and the damp cellars of the Kremlin the words of Our Lord still ring in their souls: "Do not be afraid of those who kill the body, but cannot kill the soul" (Matthew 10:28). The Communists indeed have the power to send the body to their hell, but the soul has escaped. The Communists can bend at will the man who thinks he is a beast; that is why the materialists of the Western world are like putty in the hands of Russian agents. But they cannot do that with their own people, for as they are slain they lift their eyes tranquilly to Heaven for a help and consolation as they pray their old prayers: "O God, forgive us an unforgivable people." Whether transplanted, deported, arrested, tortured, maimed or killed, these great and good people are saying to the Communist leaders with their Dostoevsky: "I would rather be wrong with Christ than right with you."

Even the Russian Communist's strong reaction against God implies God. He does not deny God, like the bourgeois atheist, or the sophomore in an American college; he challenges God; he hates God for the moment. As no one can really be lawless without law, so one cannot be anti-God without God. There is no religious indifference in the Russian soul. Never will they come under the Divine threat: "You are neither cold nor hot" (Revelation 3:15). If the Communists today choose the Devil, it is not because they want the Devil, but because their intense soul mistook him for God, for the Devil is the impersonator of God. There is no greater lie than that which looks like the Truth. They mistook what is God-like, but they do not deny God. As their own Khomiakov put it:

> "And we went to see our cure,
> Not from God, yet of His hand."

In concentration camps and under bright prison lights, the Russian soul feels what he calls a *strast,* or passion, which is the very word he uses for the Passion of Christ; he feels Calvary in his soul. Even now in Siberia, despite the vigilance of the Soviet guards, the starved and famished bodies of the Russian people have strength enough to sing from their souls the old Cossack song:

> "For us death now can hold no fear
> Our work we have accomplished well
> Siberia is conquered to Christ
> And we have not lived in vain."

How our Western world needs their virtues! their love of the soul! Oh beloved Russian people, we reach out to you our love in Christ, and pray that your land which once was Holy Russia may again bear that blessed name. Your Communist persecutors have a Fifth Column here, but you Russian people have a greater Fifth Column among all true lovers of God and His Divine Son. Millions pray every day to Our Lady of Fatima for your liberation. Every morning throughout the entire world, every priest after Mass says nine prayers for your intentions — your peace and freedom.

This year we of the Mystical Body of Christ and your Eastern Rite in Russia will celebrate Easter on the same day. Today in your liturgy is what you call your day of Forgiveness. You give up the spirit of carnival and begin your Lent a few days earlier than we — what sturdy people you are! On this day of forgiveness, in your monasteries your monks ask forgiveness of one another; in your homes and your towns you beg pardon of all whom you have offended. May we join you in this Day by asking your forgiveness for allowing the chains of slavery to enfold you. We have wronged you by our moral indifference to evil more than you have wronged us. Therefore forgive us. You have nothing to lose but your chains, but we have to lose that false tolerance that helped forge your chains.

Just as the sun picks up the moisture of the earth, gathers it in clouds and then carries it over seas and continents to drop it on another land, we beg the angels of God to catch up our prayers and waft them like clouds beyond all the iron curtains of the world, and drop them like gentle dew into your Russian *dousha,* to give it strength and courage, that as *Bogoiskateli* — or God-seekers, as you call yourselves — you may find in public and in joy the same Christ you now know in secret and in pain.

Tomorrow morning and every Monday morning during Lent, I will offer my Mass for the Russian people and every other day there will be a special remembrance. Will you start your Lent by attending Mass tomorrow in union with that intention and continue it until Easter? He who is alien to the spiritual interests of Russia is a stranger to the cause of Christ. Stir up your *dousha.* Pray in particular to the saints whom Russia venerates: St. Nicholas, St. Basil, St. John Chrysostom, SS. Cyril & Methodius. Intercede to Our Lady of Fatima! Go to Mass every morning during Lent, I beg you — and pray in the spirit of the Russian Princess whose last words as she faced the Communist firing squad were: "Prince of Peace and Lord of all, bless us with the grace of prayer and in this unbearable hour, give rest to our humble and troubled souls."

God love you!

FALLEN AWAYS

"Who among you having a hundred sheep and losing one of them would not leave the other ninety-nine in the desert and go after the lost one until he finds it?" (Luke 15:4)

Friends:

A few years ago I was receiving a convert into the Church at St. Patrick's Cathedral in New York. While she was making her profession of Faith, and saying that she believed Our Lord was the Son of the Living God, and that the Church was His Mystical Body, someone stole her umbrella. We never recovered it. Those who hate the Church would probably say that a Bishop stole it, or that I did. Let us assume that a Catholic did steal it. If such be the case, it is a beautiful illustration of the truth that not all of them will go to heaven.

Our Blessed Lord illustrates this truth, not by the example of an umbrella, but by the example of the wheat and the cockle. In His Mystical Body, the good and the bad, the umbrella thieves and the umbrella owners live together. And the Lord said: "Let them grow side by side until the harvest" (Matthew 13:30), that is, until the Judgment; then the distinction will be made clear. When we think of all the advantages that a member of Christ's Mystical Body has had, it is no wonder that when a Catholic does make a mess of it, he is apt to become worse than others. A very special term is given to those who lost the faith, that is, those who once were united by Charity to Our Lord's Mystical Body and then left it: they are called the "fallen aways." It is a little softer than "lost sheep," for they are not necessarily lost. Though without Charity, some of them still have bonds with the Mystical Body through Faith and Hope.

Why do some Catholics fall away? First I will give you two reasons why they do *not* fall away. No one ever left the Mystical Body because he wanted to lead a holier life. Secondly, no one ever left the Church for a reason, i.e., because he had difficulty with the Creed, but rather because he had difficulty with the Commandments.

Now we come to why one falls away from the Church. I said that no one ever leaves the Mystical Body of Christ for a reason: he leaves it for a thing. Our Lord in the parable of the banquet mentioned *three* things: egotism, worldliness, and sex. One man declined His invitation to His Heavenly Banquet because he had bought a farm, another because he wanted to try five pair of oxen, and the other because he had married. There is nothing wrong in buying a farm or trying five pair of oxen, or in marrying a wife. Then why did Our Lord say that "none of those who were first invited shall taste of My supper" (Luke 14:24)? Because they made these material and secondary things take precedence over the Kingdom of God and the salvation of their souls.

The first *thing* that can make souls fall away is pride in which the ego becomes so inflated with what it thinks it knows that not even God could teach it anything. Pride is often an adolescent and college phenomenon when a little knowledge goes to an empty head like wine to an empty stomach.

The second thing which solicits souls from Our Lord is worldliness. Here the soul becomes so absorbed in business, pleasures, busy-body activities, temporal security, that God is considered a pious extra. Their lives become so externalized that the inner life of the spirit perishes. To this group belongs politicians, and social climbers who give up the Church saying: "They can never get anywhere with a Cross on their backs."

The third thing for which some fall away is the flesh, or sex understood as an excessive love of carnal pleasure. The immediacy of a sensate experience takes precedence over the spirit. Sacrifice becomes more and more irksome and the body becomes the thing to be served and worshiped. It is bad behavior which creates doubts, not doubts that create bad behavior. In this group belong all those who leave the Church for the sake of a second or third marriage in open defiance of the words of Our Lord: "What God has joined let no man put asunder."

After these *things* have done their work, then comes the second step of a fallen away, namely rationalizing the fall. For example, a fallen away may say: "I no longer believe in Confession." What he means is: "I am living in sin, and since I am not prepared to give it up, I will give my guilt an intellectual coating by attacking the remedy." Or another will say: "I think belief in hell is stupid." What he means is, "I know very well that what I sow, I will reap, and since I am sowing evil, I will reap hell. But this is such an uncomfortable thought that the only way I can get peace is to deny hell." People who cannot face their true motives always try to disguise and justify them. The only difference between the rationalization of a university professor and that of a moron, is that the first can give crazier reasons.

But it is less important to know why some Catholics fall away than to know how to bring them back again to the embrace of Our Lord. The first absolute and invariable rule is: "Never, never, never argue with a fallen away." Since he did not leave for a reason, he cannot be brought back with reason. For example, to give a man arguments for the Blessed Trinity, when he is involved in a marital triangle, is to waste ammunition by shooting in the dark. If they left for pride, then the return will not come with a syllogism, but with the humility of the bended knee. If they left for worldliness, the return will come not through an argument but through a retreat and self - discipline. If they left through sex, then peace will come by leaving the occasion of sin. There is nothing harder in all the world to understand than the fulness of the Truth of Christ in His Mystical Body when one is living an evil life. But just as soon as one turns his back on evil, the truths reappear in all their clarity. A robber does not like a spotlight on him when he robs; and the man who leads an evil life hates Christ, the Light of the World.

The second rule is to understand the anguish, the misery, the unhappiness and the anxiety which pervades the soul of all those who have fallen away. He who had the faith and lost it is different from the evil man who never had it to lose. The difference is between two men going into a dark room, one of whom was once in the room before when it was lighted, the other of whom was never in it before. The first has a sense of having lost something; he has a familiarity of homeliness which begets in him a yearning to see it lighted again. The other recognizes nothing and cannot even guess his way around. Frustrated he is apt to fall and break his neck. Or, to change the figure, the difference is like the marriage of two men to two old shrews. One man was married before to a lovely, charming wife who died; the other never was married before. The first man suffers more than the second because he once knew the best. So he who loved Christ in His fulness and then fell away suffers more than the one who never loved Him.

Those who fall away from pride suffer but little, because pride is such an apparently clean sin, and the proud man often mistakes his wounds as badges of victory; those who fall away through avarice or worldliness destroy the spirit and become exactly like that which they love: material and ephemeral. But those who fall away because of the *flesh,* have a tension and a pull inside them which is terrific. This is due to the close union of body and soul in sex. When man punishes us, he takes something away; when God punishes, He leaves us alone; and nothing is more terrible in all the world than to live with our ego. It is our ego that burns in hell. Those who are outside the Church because of a bad marriage suffer an anxiety and dread which is unknown to those who never received Holy Communion. They feel disappointed in what they have, and they find that like Judas, they sold Our Lord out of all proportion to His due worth. There is a diminishing return in their pleasure, age is creeping up, the body is losing its tension. They have what we might call "black grace" or a loneliness and separateness from God. "White grace" is the Presence of God in the soul. "Black grace" is the sense of His absence, the feeling of being "without God." Whenever a man falls from God he falls on himself. That is when his ego becomes unbearable. Charles de Foucauld of France who lost his faith and later found it and became a hermit in the desert describes this inner disgust of a fallen away. "You, O God, made me feel a sorrowful void, a deep depression…. It used to come upon me every evening when I was alone in my rooms; it kept me dumb and oppressed during so-called celebrations; I organized them, but when the time came, I spent them in numbness, distaste and infinite boredom…. You gave me the vague uneasiness of a bad conscience which was all asleep and yet, not quite dead." Underneath all the ashes of these lives, there are some burning embers, and woe to us if we do not fan them with the spirit of the love of God. One thing is certain. Our Holy Faith will not prevent a person from sinning, but it will take most of the fun out of it. The unhappy conscience becomes like a toothache which says: "See the dentist." Only here, the remorse and anxiety say: "This is not the road to peace; return to the Savior."

A third rule applies to those of us who are still members of Christ's Body. We must not flatter ourselves that we are better than our fallen brother or sister. It is God Who judges the heart; we see only the face. If we suffered the same temptations as they did, perhaps our fall would have been a thousand times worse. As St. Paul warns: "Whoever thinks he is standing firmly should take care not to fall" (1 Corinthians 10:12). Furthermore, if they had the same graces and opportunities that we have had, they might have been apostles and saints.

Too often it happens that when someone sins once against chastity, others make it an excuse to sin a thousand times against charity. Sometimes Our Divine Savior punishes those who are unduly severe against sinners by withdrawing His Grace, and permitting them to fall into the very sins which they condemned in others. A false sense of moral superiority may drive them farther and farther away from Our Lord. How ashamed the righteous must have been when Paul became an Apostle, and when Augustine, the sinner, became a Saint, and when the woman at the well recognized Our Lord as Savior of the world. It is pretty hard for us who can never know what goes on in another's soul to tell which are the pigs who want to stay in the mud and which are the sheep who are trying to get out.

Those who do not want sinners forgiven and restored are with the supernatural like a dog with a bone. The Parable of the Prodigal is the story of two boys who lost their father's love; one because he was too bad, the other because he was too good. The bad boy returned, but the good boy did not want his sinful brother back again, and he is not at the banquet in the father's house. Those who would exclude others from the Body of Christ will find themselves excluded.

This is Jubilee Year of the Great Pardon! I plead with all of you who have left the Father's House to come back! Our love for you is keeping the door open!

The Good Shepherd wants you back, for He said the angels in heaven rejoice more at one fallen away returning than in the ninety-nine who remain faithful. A mother gives most attention to the child who falls the most often.

Our Blessed Mother wants you back, for she knows what it is to be without Our Lord — for she was without Him for three days!

The Eucharist Lord in the Tabernacle wants you back for He misses the sacramental kiss He once gave you in Holy Communion.

The Confessional Box wants you back, for you never could call Our Lord Savior unless you had sinned.

And you want to be back, for in your worry, your sleeplessness, your fears, you know you want that "Love you fall just short of in all love."

Never give up hope! Not until you have begun to be infinitely wicked and Our Lord ceases to be infinitely merciful, may you despair.

We will pray for you as we await your letter seeking directions back again to the Father's House.

Sometimes a reconciliation is sweeter than an unbroken friendship.

There are two ways of knowing how good God is: one is never to lose Him; the other is to lose Him and find Him again. Let that be your way.

You have one thing in your treasury which God has not, and which you alone can give Him, to make Him and you happy — your sins.

God love you!

THE CHURCH AND THE MIND

ADDRESS DELIVERED ON MARCH 12, 1950

"If the Son frees you, you will, indeed, be free."
(John 8:36)

Friends:

What would you say is the major peril in the world today? I would say it is Authoritarianism, for it not only includes Communism, but all those old and new forms of State supremacy and political dictatorship which destroy freedom.

Authoritarianism enslaves in three ways: (1) By subjecting the mind to dogmas and systems; (2) By making fear the basis of authority; (3) By destroying freedom of thought.

Our Divine Savior lived and grew up under an Authoritarian system which tyrannized His people. When therefore He began prolonging His Life to His Mystical Body the Church, He made it a bulwark against all forms of Authoritarianism, contrasting the two in these words: "You know that the rulers of the Gentiles lord it over them, and their great ones make their authority over them felt; but it shall not be that way with you. Whoever wishes to be great among you shall be your servant; whoever wishes to be first among you shall be your slave" (Matthew 20:25-27).

How thankful we should be to Our Dear Lord for saving us as members of His Mystical Body from the terrible menace of Authoritarianism. He does it in three ways: (1) Because in the Church we obey not a system, but a Person; (2) Because in the Church the basis of our obedience is not fear but love; and (3) Because in the Church our freedom of thought is saved from narrowness by knowing both sides of a question.

1. In Authoritarianism one must submit to a system, that is, to a complicated network of dogmas and assumptions, superstitions and codes, directives and orders which are always abstract and imper-sonal, such as Dialectical Materialism, or Class Con-flict or the Labor Theory of Value. But as Catholics we do not subscribe to a system of dogmas; we be-gan with a Person, namely, the Person of Jesus Christ, continued in His Mystical Body. Our Faith is the meeting of two personalities: Our Lord and you. There is no adhesion to an abstract dogma, but rather Communion with a Person Who can neither deceive nor be deceived. The Authoritarian starts with a party line; we start with Our Divine Lord, the Son of the Living God Who said: "I am the Truth." Truth therefore is Personal. As the love of a child

for its home is more than the sum of the commands of its parents, so our love for the Church is more than the sum of the Truths which express that Faith. Our Faith is, first and foremost, in Christ living in His Mystical Body and then, only secondly, in explicit beliefs. If He did not reveal them, we would not believe them. If we lost Him, we would lose our beliefs. He comes first; everything else is secondary.

There is no doctrine, no moral, no dogma, no liturgy, no belief apart from Him. *He* is the object of our Faith, and not a dogma. As the dogma that a young man should give a ring to the young lady to whom he is engaged, is secondary to his love of her as a person, so nothing to us is credible apart from Christ in His Mystical Body. If we believed that Our Lord was not God, but only a good man who lived 1900 years ago, we would never believe in the Eucharist, or the Trinity. If we believed that all Our Lord left was a few shorthand notes transcribed by secretaries over 30 years after His Death, we would not believe in the forgiveness of sins. But because we know that Our Lord once taught, governed and sanctified through a Body taken from the womb of His Mother overshadowed by the Holy Spirit, and is now living, teaching and governing today in His Mystical Body taken from the womb of humanity and overshadowed by the same Holy Spirit, we accept every single word of His, not only what His secretaries wrote but also His Memory or Tradition through these 1900 years. We want no institution standing between Our Lord and us. And His Mystical Body no more stands between Him and us than my body stands between me and my visible head or between me and my invisible mind. His Mystical Body the Church is what St. Augustine 1500 years ago, called the *Totus Christus,* the *Whole Christ.* Thank God for your Faith in the Person of the Living Christ, the Eternal contemporary. It is the hope of the world against Authoritarianism.

2. The Church, the Mystical Body of Christ saves us from Authoritarianism with its police systems and propaganda, because the basis of our Faith is not fear, but love. Because Authoritarianism is based on a system, it begets fear. Because we start with the Person of Christ in His Mystical Body, we believe not through fear, but with love. One cannot love Dialectical Materialism or Ethical Cosmopolitanism, or Pragmatic Humanism, but one can love a person. Between our created personality and His uncreated Personality there is a bond of love. So inseparable are the two that Our Lord did not communicate to Peter the power of ruling and governing His Church until three times Peter had told Our Lord that he loved Him above all else.

The submission we make to Our Savior in His Mystical Body is something like the loving submission that we make to the best and oldest and wisest of our friends, or the obedience a son gives to his father. We feel no distance between us who are taught, and the Church of Christ which teaches. As a pupil more and more absorbs the teachings of the professor, the less becomes the distance between them. There finally comes a moment when there is a partnership begotten of love for that common truth. The more we know Our Lord and obey the Truth manifested through His Body, the Church, the less we feel under Him. The more His Truth becomes ours, the more we love Him. To fall from faith in Our Lord in His Mystical Body is like falling from friendship with a person we love, to the abstract love of a book which he wrote, or a trinket which he wore. I cannot imagine anything more cold, more enslaving, more paralyzing to human reason, more destructive of freedom than that thing to which millions are prostrating every day, the terrible anonymous authority, "they." "They say." "They are wearing navy blue this year." "They say that Catholics adore Mary." "They say that hair will be shorter this year." "They say that Freud is the thing." Who are *they*? Countless slaves and puppets are bowing down daily before that invisible, tyrannical myth of "they." No wonder dictators arose to personalize that terrible slavery!

But *we know* in Whom we believe: Our Lord living in His Body! A beautiful proof of the love quality of the Church was supplied by the thousands of fallen aways who wrote within the last two weeks, and most of whom were outside the Church because of a second marriage.

They expressed themselves as miserably unhappy on the inside, suffering boredom, ennui, disgust, anxiety and unhappiness, not because they had broken a law, but because they had broken their relationship of love with the Sacred Heart. Their loneliness also bears witness to the Truth that when there is no Person to love, there is no certitude, there is only subjection. When there is love of Christ, love believes everything. The deeper the love, the greater the certitude. But since no love can surpass the love of the Living Christ prolonged in His Mystical Body, there is no greater certitude in all the world. Thank God for it! Only such love can save you from Authoritarianism with its fear, and make you both free and happy!

3. The Church, the Mystical Body of Christ, saves us from Authoritarianism because it gives us not freedom *from* thought, but freedom of thought. The Devil has pretty well convinced some of his subjects that they should not accept the Authority of Christ, because they would be weakening their reason. He suggests that any limitation put upon reason is due to a sinister cause. In the Garden he suggested that not to know evil, whether it be of the mind such as Communism, or of the body such as cancer, is to destroy freedom. So the Devil told our first parents, "The purpose of God is to prevent free

inquiry. He wants to keep the human race in ignorance. Do not be fooled. He is an old 'fuddy-duddy' and reactionary. Be liberal." God is thus made to appear as an enemy of Truth and free inquiry, in the same way that a father who refuses to let his five-year-old son have a shotgun, is said by some to be denying the freedom of the son.

The error of the Devil is that continuance in loyalty and love means discontinuance in mental growth. To the Devil, to continue to be loyal to one's wife, country, an ideal, is a mark of slavery and a want of freedom.

There is, however, *one* sense in which the Church restricts reason and that is in the same way that all Truth restricts it. Before I went to school I was free to believe that Shakespeare was born in 1224, but after a little education, I had to stop such liberalism and freedom of thought. I was also free to believe that H^2O were the initials of a spy, but the school soon became "reactionary" and put a stop to that kind of thinking by telling me it was the symbol for water.

Freedom is not in liberation *from* Truth, but in the acceptance of Truth. I am free to draw a triangle only on condition that I accept the Truth of the triangle, and give it three sides, and not in a stroke of broad-mindedness give it thirty-three sides. This is what Our Lord meant when He said: "The Truth will set you free" (John 8:32).

The relation between Divine Truth of the Church and freedom can be told in the analogy of an island in the center of the sea. On that island children danced and sang and played. One day three men came to the island in three individual rowboats. They said to the children: "Who put up these walls around the island? They are restricting your liberty. Tear them down. Be free. Throw off the shackles of dogmatic walls and moral restraints." So the children tore down the walls. Now if you go back to the island, you will find all the children huddled in the center, afraid to dance, afraid to sing, afraid to play, afraid of falling into the sea.

It is not Truth and Goodness that are narrowing, but Authoritarianism, because it never permits anyone a knowledge of what is on the outside. That is the trouble with much secular knowledge. It never knows both sides of the question. May I speak here as a professor of philosophy. I have studied at some of the finest universities in Europe and never once have I felt any restraint on my thinking. In our own Catholic University in Washington every teacher in our philosophy department knows well the teachings of Marx, Lenin, Stalin, Sartre, Heidegger, Jaspers and Freud, but alongside of these ephemeral systems he has a vast knowledge of the great tradition of common sense. He knows both sides of a question. But those in secular universities very often not only do not know the thought of the first sixteen centuries, but their courses in philosophy are merely a history of systems, not a philosophy of life. This is as unsatisfying as a man who wanted to be a doctor being taught only the history of medicine. Any teacher of philosophy in a Catholic University would know such a reference as Rep. 537A, but how many secular teachers of philosophy who study only one side of a question, know the meaning of 3d. 24a.3. q.1. ad 2? When any of our students of Philosophy pick up St. Thomas to study his proofs or the existence of God, the very first thing that meets their eyes are the reasons that great thinker gives for atheism. Think of it! His question, "Is there a God?" is prefaced by a two-fold presentation of atheistic Communism. Throughout his whole, monumental work, every single position is prefaced by the strongest objections. So strong are these objections that Voltaire the scoffer, in order to gather ammunition against the Church, spent six months copying the objections, but he never read the answers. Notice too, every Encyclical of the Church begins with a statement of the position of the adversary. A Communist once told me that the best and fairest exposition he ever saw on Communism was in the Encyclical *Divini Redemptoris*.

That is why we love the Church. It studies all sides of a problem. Our freedom is not in independence of law, but in dependence on love! No man is free who is dependent on what he does not love, whether it be his boss, his government, or his dictator. He alone is free who loves the Love Which is God.

Why is it that those who are victims to that anonymous authority "they" always say we are enslaved? The truth is, we are! We are enslaved in mind to the Incarnate Wisdom of God; we are enslaved in will, to the Love of Him Who died on the Cross that we might be reprieved of sins; we are enslaved in our choices, to Him Whose Love in the Sacraments is so ecstatic that He leaves us nothing else to love but Him. If this be slavery, and it is, I would rather be in chains with Christ, than free with them.

God love you!

THE CHURCH AND WORRIES

ADDRESS DELIVERED ON MARCH 19, 1950

"The spirit is willing, but the flesh is weak."
(Matthew 26:41)

Friends:

Never before in our history have there been as many
upset minds as there are today! As one psychologist put it: "The neurotic is the step-child of modern civilization."

Alongside of this increased mental instability
there is a decreased knowledge of the true nature
of a human being, the ignorance of which intensi-
fies the disease. The psychologist who starts with the
idea that man is only a sick cow can never restore
him to peace. To fix a watch, one must know the
nature of a watch; to explain a man to himself, one
must know the nature of a man. It is our purpose
to present the psychology of the Mystical Body of
Christ regarding the two major worries of modern
man: (1) Human frailty; (2) Worry.

Human frailty: Here is understood that state of
mind which asks: "Why did I ever do such a thing?

What made me act against my better self? I knew it was wrong when I did it, but why did I do it?"

Some psychiatrists say that the unconscious mind acts this way because when you were an infant, you loved your father too much and hated your mother, or you hated your father and loved your mother too much. This is sheer nonsense and explains nothing. The poor fathers and mothers get blamed for everything by the sex psychiatrists. It is about time for parents to rebel against the insinuation that they are responsible for everything little John and Mary do!

The true explanation of life is this: Man is composed of (1) soul or mind, (2) body or flesh, (3) his environment which is the world about him. The mind was meant to know all truth; the body was meant to enjoy its pleasures for the sake of the soul; and the world was made to serve the body and soul for the sake of God! That is the true order.

The Church tells us that, due to an abuse of freedom, human nature became disordered or eccentric in the sense of being thrown off-center, like planets which get out of their orbit. The result was that there is left in every man an impulse to consider each of these, the mind, the body, or the world in isolation from one another and from God. For example, there is a tendency on the part of the mind to exalt the ego into infinity and make itself a god, independent of all law, authority and morality. This is what is known as the concupiscence of Egotism, or Pride. There is a second impulse on the part of the body which prompts it to enjoy the pleasures of the flesh apart from right reason and the law of God. This is the concupiscence of Sex. The third impulse is the tendency to use the world, not as a means to God, but as an end in itself. This is called the concupiscence of false security, or Avarice. If you want a high sounding name for these *concupiscences,* you may call them with the psychologists, *libidos.*

The Church further tells us that they are like three little gremlins down in the cellar of our minds, and that they are constantly trying to come upstairs to disturb the household of reason. But they are also clever enough to disguise themselves. Egotism never says: "Be proud." It whispers: "My, you are smart since you went to college. You do not need a God to teach you, or a moral law to guide you." Sex never says: "Commit adultery." It whispers: "Read Freud." "Beware of repression." "Be self-expressive." False security never says: "Be greedy." It whispers: "The only purpose of life is to make money, and if you can't take it with you, don't go."

In contrast, notice how wise and scientific is Catholic psychology on the subject of man's impulses. The major psychologies of the world are narrow in the sense that they acknowledge only one impulse to the exclusion of the others. One type of psychology reduces everything to sex, another to the desire of significance; another to security. But no one considers all three as does the Church. Man has three wells into which he can fall — that is why the psychologists are narrow minded. They think the only well is the one into which they have fallen.

Reducing it to the practical, the Church's position can be summarized in points: (1) Do not be alarmed because you are tempted to do wrong. There would be something wrong with you if you were not tempted. (2) The temptations do not prove you are wicked; they only prove you are human. (3) You are not intrinsically corrupt, otherwise you would not be disturbed by suggestions of evil. You are never tempted beyond your strength. (4) With every resistance to temptation in Christ's Name, you acquire merit for Heaven. That is how you prove your love of God, by choosing Him and His Law to something else. (5) By constant resistance to temptation you become self-possessed, which is the condition of inner peace, not other-possessed as is the alcoholic, the sex-maniac and the materialist.

The Church recommends the practice of three virtues to overcome the three libidos: (1) Humility, to conquer egotism, which makes us think we are better than others. (2) Chastity, to conquer sex, by realizing that the body is for the Lord. (3) Almsgiving, kindness and charity to temper our acquisitiveness and greed. If you were sick you would send for a physician. Since you are weak, call on the Lord.

The second major worry is *Boredom*. It is frightening to see the vast number of our young people bored with life before they have started to live. So many of the married are bored too, either because they are loved too much and suffer satiety and fed-upness, or because they are loved too little and feel ennui and are dissatisfied.

The Psychology of the Church explains this boredom in three ways.

1. The Church teaches that man is composed of body and soul, the finite and the infinite. So long as man is on this earth, he feels the pull of both, and may be likened to a mountain climber half-way up the craggy heights. Above is the peak of the infinite to which he aspires; below is the abyss of failure into which there is the danger of falling. In this life man is in a state of suspension. Only Perfect Life, Truth and Love can satisfy him. Therefore he is restless until he rests in God!

2. The Church tells us that boredom increases in direct ratio to the loss of the purpose of life, namely the saving of our immortal soul. This accounts for the boredom of the young, however well they are educated. They no sooner set out on the seas of life, than they are disgusted with the journey. No wonder! Could anything be more unbearable than to sail into an awful void, not knowing where we are going, or whether there was another shore?

The bored are like the prodigal son who ran away from the Father's home. He was right in being hungry; he was wrong in living on the husks that were given to the swine. So the bored are right in craving for more love and more truth and more life than they have. They are miserable and unhappy and wrong because they are trying to satisfy the infinite by living on husks, as if they were made only to breathe, mate and die. They think that if one husband or wife does not satisfy, another will. But all they are adding is zeros. If a cup of salt water does not satisfy, a barrel full will not. They feel as if they were being suffocated, which is nothing else than the depressing distress of being separated from God. They are breathing in the same air they breathe out. This is the boredom of humanism.

3. The Church tells us that God permits the soul to be anxious, frustrated and bored when it turns from Him, in order that it may come back to Him. By constantly stirring the waters of the soul with His Finger, He prevents false peace so that in our disgust and restlessness we might throw ourselves on His Sacred Heart. Ennui is a hunger for the Infinite; boredom is a longing for God; disenchantment is a desire for the ecstatic love of God.

The difference between those who have faith in God and those who have not can be told in this comparison. A child is given a ball to play with and told that it is the only ball that he will ever have in his life; he knows that someday it will wear out, that it may be punctured, or possibly may even be stolen. From that point on, the child will never again enjoy the ball thoroughly, but will be bored with it. He cannot play with it too much, otherwise it will wear out; he must live in mortal dread of losing it.

Suppose now that one day as he contemplates his single ball, some one comes to him and says: "Here is another ball, which is yours on one condition; that you use the ball you have according to all the rules of the game. Then you will be given another ball, maybe in a few years, maybe next month, maybe tomorrow. This new ball will be the best ball that was ever made; it will make you happy every time you pick it up; it is something you will want to play with forever." The natural reaction of the child will be to stop worrying about his first ball. He can even now begin to enjoy it, because he knows that even if he loses it, he will have another.

The first ball stands for this world. Those who think they are like monkeys have only one world. They cannot enjoy it too much because they are afraid of growing too old to play with it, or of the ball being punctured by wars and depressions. Some become so fearful of death, and losing the only world they know, that they cover up their worry with alcoholism, sleeping tablets, scepticism and cynicism. But those who have the faith and a complete philosophy of life, can not only enjoy this world while they have it, but they live in beautiful hope of that other world where God is the voluptuousness of the pure.

The world to the Catholic is like a scaffolding up through which souls climb to the Kingdom of Heaven. When the last soul has climbed up through that scaffolding to fill the places vacated by the fallen angels, then the scaffolding shall be torn down and burned with fire, not because it is base, but simply because it has done its work. It has brought us back again to God.

If you are weak and frail the Church bids you not to be discouraged. If your flesh and blood are inclined to evil, the Church will give a transfusion of Divine Flesh and Blood in the Eucharist, to overcome your weakness. If you are bored, remember that you could never be bored if you were not made for something more than the finite. A pig is never bored with his sty, nor a swallow with his nest, but man can be bored in his own home. This is because he is really on pilgrimage back again to God.

If then you have reached a moment of life where you have had a relatively happy marriage, have been successful, and yet are still worried on the inside, let me tell you; it is God Who is torturing your soul. In the evening of your life He is creating inner discontent that you may break the shell of your egotism, and begin to live on a new level of life with Him!

Freud, the sex-mad psychiatrist took as the inspiration of his books these words of a Latin poet: "If I cannot move the gods on high, I shall set all hell in an uproar." And that he has done; the inner hell of unconsciousness. May I beg you who are frustrated, unhappy, miserable, and anxious to get out of that inner hell by emptying that hell through confession and by filling your soul with the Bread of Life and the Wine that nourishes Virgins!

Shepherdless souls, I plead with you! Away with those who would define you by what is *lowest* in you, your glands, your sex, your sensuality! Learn the psychology of the Mystical Body of Christ, which defines you by what is *best* and *highest* in you, by your image and likeness to the God Who made you.

The world defines you by your environment; Our Lord defines you by your destiny! Taste and see that the Lord is sweet!

Some people say we have our hell on this earth; we do! But not all of it; we just start it here! So it is with Heaven! We start Heaven here too! And if I could only get one soul in the radio audience to overcome worries by loving God with his whole heart and mind and strength, I would be the happiest man in the world!

God love you!

THE CHURCH AND SIN

ADDRESS DELIVERED ON MARCH 26, 1950

"Whose sins you forgive are forgiven them,
and whose sins you retain are retained."
                                    (John 20:23)

Friends:

It is only fair to warn the goody-goodies who deny there is any such thing as sin, that sin is our subject today. It is not true, as these holy innocents say, that anyone who thinks of sin has a guilt complex, any more than a person who is sick has a physician complex, or a housewife whose pantry is empty has a grocery-store complex. The fact is: sinners do sin.

There are two ways of knowing sin; those who have faith, know sin in its cause; those who have no faith, know sin in its effects.

For those who know God and make some attempt to love Him, sin is known in its cause; that is, as the breaking of a relationship of love. Life's greatest tragedies come from hurting those whom we love, and since God is supreme Love, sin is felt as lovelessness. Many can remember their childhood days, when a parent pretended he did not love, and how the little child-heart broke and the world seemed to dissolve at that severing of the bond of affection. That is the way a member of Christ's Mystical Body feels when he estranges himself from that Love, Which once known, he can never live without. He is miserable and unhappy until communion is restored.

On the other hand, those who have no faith and who deny the moral law know sin by its effects. Guilt comes out not only in the body, but in the mind in various forms of psychoses and neuroses, all of which are symptoms of the inner guilt. They deny the reality of sin, but they cannot deny the reality of its effects. I may deny the law of gravitation, but if I throw myself from the Empire State Building, I am not free to escape the effects of my denial. So a man is free to be an atheist, but he is not free to escape the effects of loneliness and hatred which atheism implies. One man who boasted of his atheism, his immorality, and his contempt for the moral law, still did not escape the effects of guilt. It came out in an insane jealousy of his wife, whom he accused of infidelity and crime.

He was unconsciously making his wife the substitute for the moral law and righteousness. But in order to cover up his own repudiation of morality, he accused his wife of doing the very things of which he was guilty.

The Christian's consciousness of sin is an open

wound; the pagan's unconsciousness of sin is like a cancer. In the days of faith, people sinned as they do now, but they knew they sinned! They broke the law, but admitted the law was right; and they knew the only way they could come back was not to make their sin honorable, but to confess it and do penance. Their sins were all like open wounds which looked as if they had been cut with a razor; obviously rent, manifestly disordered but the blood healthy.

But those who say that guilt is a complex derived from a primitive taboo, and that sin is a metaphysical spook to frighten people, are like a person with a hidden cancer which does not manifest itself until it is too late to cure. They go along in their unbelief, boasting of their moral goodness, and then all of a sudden, they are stricken down with compulsion neuroses, become split personalities, develop fear fantasies, and finally end in that despair and loneliness which is a foretaste of hell.

When a civilization sins and denies that it sins, it becomes necessary for God to make it feel the *effects* of sin. Just as some people do not know they are working too hard until their health begins to break, so some souls can never come to the *consciousness* of sin unless they feel the *consequences* of sin. That is why we ought to be so much worried about our modern world. Divorces, murders, godless education, carnal license, slander, and selfishness; all these sins are committed with utter abandon. There is only one way our world can be made to realize how much it has departed from the Foundation of Divine Life, and that is by being made to feel the effects of sin in catastrophe and crisis. Will God use Russia now as He once used Assyria as the "rod of His anger"?

As ruined health in body and mind is the *physical* result of alcoholism; as a broken home is the *moral* result of infidelity and divorce; so is chaos the *historical* result of a Godless civilization. We must not think that God arbitrarily brings disaster upon us as a parent might spank a child for disobedience. (Only people over fifty can remember the phenomenon of spanking. Incidentally, there is nothing that develops character like a pat on the back, provided it is given often enough, hard enough, and low enough.) Rather, disaster and catastrophe flow from violation of the moral law of God, as thunder follows lightning, and as ignorance follows laziness. God made the world in such a way that sin produces certain effects, and these chaotic historical moments are the Divine Judgment on the way we live.

Every sinner feels remorse, boredom and fear. In relation to the past, there is remorse; in relation to the present, boredom; in relation to the future, fear! The Sacrament of Penance rids us of these three:

1. Lest the remorse of past sins seep deep into unconsciousness and become the hidden springs of

mental kinks, the Church long before psychiatry was ever thought of, laid down this law: No serious sin must ever be repressed more than twelve months. If, therefore, any member of the Church does not bring up his submerged guilt to the level of consciousness within one year, he is out of the Church! The Church orders her children to avoid repression by lifting out of the dark, deep cellars of unconsciousness, those unrecognized, unfaced guilts and habits of sin which threaten to become embedded, thus producing eccentricities, and nerves, and spoiled personality. The Church also knew that if repressed guilt was let go, men might become determinists and excuse themselves saying that they could not help being that way. They might put the blame on their mother or father as some psychoanalysts do. The Church, on the contrary, says: "Face this deed as your own; acknowledge it as an act of your own free will. Be a man, not a Freudian! Moral repression will drive you mad; confess your sins by throwing yourself into the arms of your Merciful Savior."

2. Secondly, the Church deals with sin in the present by removing the cause of boredom and anxiety through self-avowal and reconciliation. Boredom is dislocation from the Divine; it is something like lonesomeness, which is due to the severance of the bonds of sympathy and love! Once the disorder of the past is brought to the surface, Our Divine Lord

offers a remedy for this boredom in confession, where our guilt is owned, that it may be disowned as we are restored to His love.

When the stomach gets a foreign substance into it which it cannot assimilate, it throws it off; this is its purgation or confession. It is just as natural for a burdened mind to purge itself through self-avowal. The dignity of personality is thus respected because, in the confessional, one becomes his own prosecuting attorney, and his own attorney for the defense. One confesses not a state of mind, but a state of conscience; and not for the purpose of having guilt explained away, but for the purpose of having it forgiven by Him Who said: "If your sins are as scarlet, they shall be made white as snow."

But why did Our Lord, in instituting this Sacrament, give this power of forgiveness to human members of the Mystical Body in Holy Orders? Why did He not tell us to bury our head in our own handkerchief and tell Him we are sorry? Well, just try crying in your handkerchief when a motorcycle cop arrests you for speeding! How easy life would be if we could have all our sins forgiven by carrying around a legal Kleenex for violating civil law, and a moral Kleenex with lace embroidery for violating Divine Law. Since Our Lord, Who is God Incarnate, forgave sins through a human nature, it is only natural to expect that through other human natures He would continue to do it in the Mystical Body. But there is another reason for telling sins to a priest. Every sin is an offense not only against God, but also against our brothers and sisters in the Mystical Body. This is very evident in a sin such as stealing, but it is no less true for even the most secret sin, for it diminishes the content of charity in the Church, as a paralyzed arm lessens the life-content of a physical body. Since, then, we offend both God and the fellowship of Christ in the Mystical Body, it is fitting that a representative of that fellowship would restore us not only back again to God, but also to the community of which Christ is the Head.

Many people sing in their bath, not because the marble of the small room give resonance to their voices, but above all else because of the joys of purification. That is the way a soul feels after a good confession. It is so happy it could sing at the thrill of getting a fresh start in life.

3. The Church overcomes fear with regard to the future by taking account of the difference between forgiveness of sin and penalty for sin. Suppose I stole your watch. I am sure you would forgive me, but you would also say: "Give me back my watch." And if I did not return it, it would prove that I lacked the condition of forgiveness, namely, reparation for the wrong which I did. If an alcoholic is converted and reformed, his sins are forgiven, but he may still have his bad liver. God forgives him when he repents, but the punishment remains. Sup-

pose every time one sins, one drives a nail into a board, and every time one is forgiven, a nail is pulled out. The board is still full of holes. The penalty for sin endures in the future, even after the sin is remitted. In confession after the priest pronounces the words of absolution, he always gives what is called a *penance,* that is, some reparation, atonement, or sacrifice to make up for the sin. No one wants to be "let off," when he has done wrong! All children feel *in more ways than one,* that when they are punished, the wrong is wiped out. Fear is banished to just the extent we do penance, as fear of a creditor vanishes with the payment of the debt.

This explains the peculiar psychology of good Catholics who bear up not only humbly under the penance imposed, but under all the trials and sufferings of life! There is not a single boy or girl in any parochial school in the United States who ever sits down in a dentist's chair without "offering up" the pain in union with the sufferings of Our Lord on the Cross. Thousands upon thousands on sick beds, wracked with fever and buffeted by pain are daily, hourly, and every minute accepting the bitterness of life in remission not only for their own sins, but for the sins of the world. They know they can act as stewards in making up for those who sin and do not pay the penalty. Pain is unbearable without love, but love can lessen pain, and most of all when it is seen coming from the Love Who suffered on a Cross and on whose Eternal Heart we can lean with joy.

When we confess our sins and do penance, we sometimes falsely think that there is a change in God; that before He was the God of Wrath, and now is the God of Love. That is not true. The change is in us, not Him. When we are in sin, we project the punishment which we know we deserve to God, thus making Him appear as Wrath. When we confess and do penance for our sins, there is no longer a fear, and God then appears as He really is: the God of Love.

Have you ever noticed that as you walk away from the light, your shadow lengthens? So it is with souls that turn away from the God of Light. After a while, they are pursuing nothing but shadows and fantasies, which are so mistaken for the real self that they hire psychoanalysts to help them chase their shadows. But as we walk to the Light of Christ the shadows fall behind. If you are unhappy, there is only one reason for it — you are unloved. As a ray of sunshine would be miserable if cut off from the sun, so is the sinful soul without God. It is no great mystery why anyone should love us! The mystery is why we should be loved. But when the world no longer loves us, and we no longer hardly love ourselves, there is only One left Who is willing to love us when all loves are ended, and that is Our Dear Lord. There has to be a God — otherwise so many people would be unloved!

Much of the mental misery of minds today comes from the awful burden of past sins, for which God's pardon has never been asked nor repentance made. May I ask all Catholics to throw themselves on the Mercy of God in Confession. Our Divine Lord said: "I came not to call the just, but sinners." He leaves the ninety-nine sheep in the field to find the one who is lost; He told us how, like the woman, He rejoices more at the one piece of money that is found, than at the possession of the nine which were never lost. A mother rejoices more at the recovery of the health of one of her sick children than in the continued health of the rest of the family.

Do not despair, no matter what your life has been. He Who forgave Magdalene will forgive you, if you humble yourself as she did and fill the house with the odor of your virtues. You have a better chance of salvation if you are a sinner wanting to be done with sin, than you have if you deny sin or think you are holier than others. As Our Lord said: "The harlots and the publicans will enter the Kingdom of Heaven before the Scribes and Pharisees."

Remember the penitent thief, who from his cross asked Our Dear Lord to forgive him. Immediately the Savior answered: "This day you shall be with Me in Paradise." And the thief died a thief, for he stole Paradise! And this is our hope — Heaven can be stolen again!

God love you!

OUR BLESSED MOTHER

ADDRESS DELIVERED ON APRIL 2, 1950

"When Jesus saw His mother there, and the disciple, too, whom He loved, He said to the disciple, 'This is your mother.'" (John 19:26, 27)

Friends:

There is only one mother in the history of the world of whom men have spoken unkindly! No one has ever heard a vicious word against the mother of Mohammed, nor Confucius, nor the mother of Hitler or Stalin; nor has anyone ever uttered a spiteful word against the mother of Judas. But oh! How tongues have slandered and how pens have splattered that lovely and beautiful Mother of Jesus! Such lies as "Catholics adore Mary," or "Catholics regard her as a goddess," are repeated almost with fiendish glee! What has this poor mother done to be so wronged, so hated and so neglected?

Just suppose you could have pre-existed your own mother, and that you had the power to fashion her according to your ideals. Would you not have made her, not only the most beautiful woman who ever lived, but also the sweetest character that ever stroked the head of a child? Do you think Our Divine Lord would have done otherwise? He Who is the Son of God pre-existed His own mother, as an artist pre-exists his painting. When Whistler finished that magnificent portrait of his mother and was complimented by a friend for his artistry, Whistler answered: "You know how it is; one tries to make his 'mummy' just as nice as one can."

If an artist who pre-exists the painting of his mother would make her beautiful, how much more should the Son of God make His Mother beautiful, as only God knows how to make a mother beautiful! God labored for a long time making a Garden of Paradise in which would be celebrated His creative masterpiece; the nuptials of man and woman! How much more should the Heavenly Father labor in preparing His re-creative masterpiece, the incarnation of His Divine Son by making a Garden that would be so free from the weeds of sin, that the Heavenly Father would not blush at sending His Son into it, a Garden against whose portals the Serpent of evil would coil in vain, a Garden in which would be celebrated the great nuptials, not of man and woman, but God and man in the Person of Our Lord and Savior, Jesus Christ. And this "flesh-girt Paradise" to be gardenered by the Adam new, this new Eden of the Incarnation, was the Woman whom

Jesus chose for a Mother — Mary, the one so stainless that an angel saluted her as "full of grace."

When a mother carries a child, there is begotten a physical and psychological bond between the two which is so inseparable that Scripture asks: "Can a mother forget her infant, be without tenderness for the child of her womb?" (Isaiah 49:15). For nine months the God-Man took up His abode in her, so that the wheat she ate and the wine she drank became as a natural Eucharist for her child, Jesus; her body became a kind of ciborium for Him Who is the Host of the world. In virtue of this should there not be a bond created between them that would endure, not through time alone, but through the agelessness of eternity? As this Mother could not forget the Child of her womb, neither could the Child forget the Mother Whom He Himself had made. As in Heaven the Son is like the Father, so on earth the Son is like the Mother. No sweeter picture is there than that of a mother looking down to the babe in her arms and pointing to the Heaven from which he came. But here for the first time a Woman holding a Babe looked not up, but down to Heaven, for Heaven was in her arms. Every other mother rears her son for herself, but here was a Mother who raised her Son for the world! The Mother and Babe are inseparable! As we cannot go to a statue of a Mother holding a Babe and hack away the Mother without destroying the Babe, so neither can we ignore the Mother, whom Jesus loved above all the creatures of earth, without hurting the Babe!

Suppose when I was invited into your house I completely ignored your mother, failed to greet her on entering, and never once addressed a word to her about you whom I claimed as a friend? Would not that be an insult to one whom you love? But must not Our Divine Lord suffer the same bitter disappointment when we refuse to show some respect to His Beloved Mother? And all the more so because of the way His life was bound up with hers, and how He willed that her life be bound up with us.

This is evident from the close relationship between the Marriage Feast of Cana and the Crucifixion! At Cana, the Gospel mentions the Mother of Our Lord before mentioning Him, saying: "And the mother of Jesus was there. Jesus was also invited" (John 2:1, 2). The wine gave out at the wedding party, probably due to the fact that Our Lord brought along all his disciples. The one who should have first noticed the shortage, and therefore the embarrassment of the guests, was the winesteward. But the Mother of Our Lord was actually the first, as if she anticipates our needs before we are aware of them! She tells Our Lord in such a simple way, as if very conscious of His Divine Power: "They have no wine" (John 2:3). She knew He could supply the deficiency! She was asking Our Lord to work His first miracle, to begin His Mission of Redemption, to launch the salvation of the world, and to proclaim Himself the Son of the Living God.

The answer of Her Divine Son went back to the very beginning of the Scriptures, when after the fall of man, God, promising a Savior, said to the Devil: "I will establish enmity between you and the woman, between your offspring and hers" (Genesis 3:15). Now the centuries had whirled away, and the fulness of time had come, for here at a village marriage feast stood *the Woman* and her *offspring*, Jesus Christ, true God and true Man. The more forcibly to drive home the lesson that as man fell through a woman, so a woman should assist in the redemption of man, Our Divine Lord now addresses her by that title of Universal Motherhood; He calls her *Woman*! She was His Mother, yes! But now that she had asked for His first public manifestation of Divine Power, He implies that she becomes bound up with all those whom He would redeem! Now she is Mother of Christ, but when redemption would be completed, she would be *the Woman,* the Mother not only of Christ but also Our Mother.

Our Divine Lord further hinted that her relationship to Him changes when He begins the work of salvation by suggesting: "What is mine, is yours; we are in this together, my Dear Mother!" He warned her that if He worked that miracle it would be the beginning of His Crucifixion and His Death. "My Hour has not yet come." Our Lord spoke at Cana of His Cross in terms of "My Hour." He very often uses that word in relation to His Passion and Death. For example, when His enemies attempted to stone Him, Sacred Scripture says: "And no man laid hands on Him, because His Hour had not yet come" (John 7:30). The night before He died, in the very shadow of the Cross, He prayed to His Heavenly Father: "Father, the Hour has come" (John 17:1). A little while later He said to the betraying Judas, who let loose the full tide of sin's rebellion: "But this is your hour, and the time for the power of darkness" (Luke 22:53). And now at Cana, for the first time He uses the expression: "My Hour has not yet come."

In other words, He says: "Do you realize, Dear Mother, that as My Heavenly Father has already sent Me on the work of redemption, you are adding your will to His and sending Me to the Cross? Once I change water into wine, an Hour will come, when in death, the wine will be changed into blood. Knowing this, do you still want to send Me to Calvary for the healing of the hearts of men? Is it your will to become the Woman, the Mother of men, as you are now the Mother of Me?"

The answer of Our Blessed Mother was startling in its sacrifice. She now speaks the last of her seven recorded utterances in Sacred Scripture. Turning to the wine stewards, she says: "Do whatever He tells you" (John 2:5). What a beautiful valedictory! She never speaks again in the Bible though the Bible speaks of her. What need is there for the moon, when the sun has risen? What further warrant for words, when the Word has spoken? She has only one mission in life; to make us do the Will of Her Divine Son. "Do whatever He tells you." As her first utterance was submission to the Divine Will in the Annunciation: "Behold the handmaid of the Lord; be it done unto me according to your word" (Luke 1:38), so her last word to us is, "Do whatever my Son wants you to do." Mary takes nothing for herself; she is not the wall where our prayers stop; she is the window through which Christ comes to us, and through which we go back to Christ. She is the stem, not the rose; she is the cloud, not the rain; she is the ciborium, not the Host; she is the sweet temptress, undoing Eve; she delivers us not to Satan, but to her Divine Son.

> "With the starry treachery
>   of thine eyes
> Tempt us back to Paradise."

Our Blessed Mother at Cana really sent her Son to the Cross; she broke her own mother-heart by speeding Him onto the battlefield of Calvary. Mothers have been lauded in song for saying: "I did not raise my boy to be a soldier," but here is a Mother who did. She raised Him to be a Redeemer. She would lose her Son in battle, not by accident, but by design. It was her will that He begin a life of sacrifice that would end in His Death.

Finally, when the Hour does come, and Our Lord is unfurled like a wounded eagle upon the Cross, He speaks to the best and dearest of all His creatures, to His Mother, and the beloved disciple, John. In this second Annunciation, in which not an angel but Our Lord speaks, He addressed her by that title which goes back to the beginning of the human race; He calls her *Woman,* the Universal Mother, the new Eve! Then a second later, comes the answer to the question: Did Mary have other children besides Our Lord? No, not according to the flesh. But was she destined to have other children according to the spirit? Most certainly! She brought forth her first born Jesus in joy. Now she begins bringing forth her other children in martyrdom and sorrow, as Our Lord says to her of John: "This is your son" (John 19:27). Our Lord then speaks to John, but He does not call him John, for if He did, he would have been only the son of Zebedee but no one else. In his anonymity John stood for all of us as Our Lord commended him to His own Mother saying: "This is your Mother." And Scripture tells us "from that hour the disciple took her into his home" (John 19:27).

Not by any metaphor, or figure of speech, nor by any legal fiction, but in virtue of the sufferings of Calvary, where she is recorded as standing at the foot of the Cross; we might even say in virtue of the pangs of childbirth, Mary became the Mother of us all whom He redeems as she was already the Mother of Him Who is the Redeemer.

As she was sent ahead to mother the Physical Body of Christ, so she was left behind for a time to mother the Mystical Body of Christ, for Scripture tells us that on the day of Pentecost, when the Mystical Body of Christ the Church was made evident to the world, she was in the midst of the Apostles, abiding in prayer.

I have never found that anyone who loved my mother, loved me less, have you? Why do you think Our Lord should be loved less because we love His Mother and on the entirely different plane? If Our Lord thought that He would be less adored because we loved His Mother, do you think He would have said to us from the Cross: "This is your Mother." But have you not always found it true, that those who *did not* love your mother, never really loved you? Think you that it should be otherwise with Our Lord Who made His own Mother?

But you ask, why such love, such devotion, so many hymns and Aves, and such tenderness? For only one reason — because she formed Christ in her, we think that she knows how to form Christ in us. That is why we love Mary, because we want to be Christlike. We believe that she has the secret. Since she knows more about her Son than anyone, we ask her to teach us how to love and serve Him.

In the language of Mary Dixon Thayer,* I pray:

> Lovely Lady dressed in blue —
>   Teach me how to pray!
> God was just your little Boy,
>   Tell me what to say!
>
> Did you lift Him up, sometimes,
>   Gently, on your knee?
> Did you sing to Him the way
>   Mother does to me?
>
> Did you hold His Hand at night?
>   Did you ever try
> Telling stories of the world?
>   O! And did He cry?
>
> Do you really think He cares
>   If I tell Him things —
> Just little things that happen?
>   And
>   Do the angels' wings
> Make a noise? Can He hear
>   Me if I speak low?
> Does He understand me now?
>   Tell me — for you know!
>
> Lovely Lady dressed in blue —
>   Teach me how to pray!
> God was just your little Boy.
>   And, you know the way!

God love you!

---

* Poem *To Our Lady* by Mary Dixon Thayer in "A Child on His Knees." — Courtesy, Macmillan Co., New York. Used by permission.

EASTER

ADDRESS DELIVERED ON APRIL 9, 1950

> *"Who will roll back the stone for us from the*
> *entrance to the tomb?"*   (Mark 16:3)

Friends:

When our Lord surrendered His Spirit to the
Heavenly Father on Good Friday, and was cold like
all dead men, and with a heart that beat no more,
friends who had shut themselves up in their houses,
and anonymous admirers who hid their light under a bushel, now began to appear. They were not
with Him in His agony, when He needed them, but
they were with Him in His death, as weavers of
wreathes, as weepers of glittering tears, and as eu-
logists of the dead. One of these friends was Joseph
of Arimathea, who secretly loving the Savior, was
yet not bold enough to declare it while He was alive.
He now would diminish his remorse by providing
a tomb for his executed friend. This rich councilor
boldly went to Pilate and asked to have the body of
Jesus. Joseph's purpose was to save Our Blessed

Lord from a dishonorable burial, i.e., from being cast into a dump, where criminals were thrown and sometimes burned.

Pilate was surprised that Our Lord was already dead, and sent for the centurion to give an official verdict concerning His death. After Pilate heard the report of the centurion, he granted the request of Joseph of Arimathea. Joseph then goes back to Calvary, takes Our Lord down from the Cross, wraps Him in a winding-sheet which he had bought, and they lay Him in a tomb cut out of a rock. A stranger's tomb alone was fitting for Him Who is a stranger to Death.

During the eating of the Paschal Lamb, the news had spread that Our Blessed Lord had been given an honorable burial by Joseph, the rich man. Like a bolt out of the blue, the Pharisees run to Pilate to protest against the delivery of the body to Joseph. As they claimed His Life, so they would claim His Death. Once in Pilate's presence, they said, "Sir, we remember that this impostor, while still alive, said, 'After three days I will be raised up!' Give orders then, that his tomb be secured until the third day, lest his disciples come and steal him away and say to the people, 'He has been raised from the dead.' This last imposture would be worse than the first" (Matthew 27:63-65).

Pilate was angry and retorted: "The guard is yours; go secure it as best you can." With the double guard of the Romans and the Pharisees, Scripture now tells us, "So they went and made the tomb secure by fixing a seal to the stone and setting the guard."

They insured against fraud in two ways. First of all, the stone which they placed there was, in the language of the Gospels, "exceedingly large," and secondly, it was sealed. This would prevent anyone from touching the body.

In the history of the world, there was never a more ridiculous spectacle than that of a hundred soldiers stationed to keep an eye on a corpse. No other grave on the face of the earth was ever watched because the dead man said that He could rise in three days. But here guards are set, lest the dead walk, the silent speak, and the pierced heart quicken to the throb of life. They say He is dead; they know He is dead; they will tell you that He will not rise again; *but still they watch.* They called Our Lord a deceiver. Will He still deceive? Has He deceived them into believing that He Who lost the battle will really win the war?

This unheard of folly of guarding a tomb beautifully describes the world situation today, in Russia and the modern soul. Russia has started with the idea of Nietzsche that God is dead, meaning religion is at an end. The basis of Communism is that religion is the invention of Capitalism to support personal ownership of property. But once private property is destroyed, Communism says religion will no longer be necessary. But Russia has had no Capitalism since 1917; there is no man there forty years of age who was ever taught religion.

But if God is dead, and religion is a myth, and faith is the opium of the people, then why do they guard the tomb, set the seal, propagandize against religion, murder priests, exile the faithful, de-humanize the Stepinacs and the Mindszentys? Why Article 124 of the Soviet constitution, forbidding all religious propaganda? Why the burning of all religious books in the Eastern zone of Berlin, if faith is dead? They do not propagandize against the Czar, nor guard the tomb of a Trotsky; why then do they set a million guards to watch what they believe is a tomb? If Christ in His Church is dead, then why fear a Resurrection? Why do they broadcast against an illusion, stand guard over corruptions, sentinel a tomb, propagandize against cadavers, pierce a fantasy with a spear, shoulder arms for an illusion, resist ghosts walking in the night, shout at the coinage of a brain?

Russia! You are sealing the tomb of a dead man, and for only one reason in the world; because you fear a Resurrection. You fear that somehow despite all of the guards, on another Easter, you will be struck dumb and the Risen Christ will be seen on the wings of a morning. As you look around you this Spring you see the dumb violets rising from the earth, telling their secrets to the sun and air. They tell you that another Resurrection is surrounding you, and that one day the Risen Christ, Whom you thought to be dead, will be walking in the light to chant a requiem over your graves, and make Russia once again holy Russia, believing in the Christ Who is the Resurrection and the Life!

What is going on in Russia is also transpiring in modern minds. To them, too, God is dead. His Moral Commandment: "Thou shalt not kill," they believe is dead, as men appropriate to themselves the taking of human life under the name of Euthanasia. Christian morality of marriage they believe to be dead, too, as divorce snaps its finger at the Divine Command: "What God has joined let no man put asunder."

Education believes that religion is dead, as students are taught that man is not God's image but only a physiological bag filled with psychological libido.

But if God is dead, and Christ is buried forever like all men, why do they take the trouble to roll stones before His grave? Why do they say to the Freudians: "Set guard over our conscience, lest the sense of guilt come to haunt us in the night; tell us that God is nothing but a development of an Oedipus father complex and will pass away with analysis"?

If God is dead, why do they say to the intelligentsia: "Seal that grave of Christ; speak to us of evolution and beasts of primeval jungles, lest there be a resurgence in our consciousness of the Christ that we have buried there"?

Why if Christ in His Mystical Body is dead, do they write, publish, smear, attack the Church, and point to the spots in the sun to prove that the sun no longer gives its light?

Thus the modern conscience represents the most stupid spectacle of the world; not soldiers and centurions, but philosophers, skeptics, agnostics and Freudian psychoanalysts, standing guard over the tomb of the dead Christ, lest He rise to be a threat and challenge to their evil lives.

I tell you! They are frantically afraid of a Resurrection. They might just as well guard against the sunrise. Their guards will be struck dumb; their seals will be broken; their rocks rent; Christ will arise in their consciences and they will be lovers again!

We who boast of the faith need the lesson, too. Many of us are like Magdalene who, though knowing that He is the Resurrection and the Life nevertheless came to anoint a dead body with spices. When she approaches the tomb, she asks: "Who will roll back the stone for us from the entrance to the tomb?" (Mark 16:3). So we, seeing 800 million people under the heel of the anti-Christ, with Calvarys erected through Eastern Europe, and the Church itself living its hour of uncrowning, are tempted to ask Magdalene's question in modern language: "Who shall lift the iron curtain from the door of the tomb of the Church?"

The Resurrection of the Mystical Body of Christ will come most likely as it did the first Easter, through the double ceremony in which Heaven and earth figured; Christ rose from the dead when the earth quaked and Heaven sent an angel to roll away the stone. Will our generation see this same conjunction of an earthly catastrophe and an outpouring of Heaven's Power, before Christ in His Mystical Body walks triumphant again over the earth? Will the new era begin with the coming of the Cossacks and the coming of the Holy Spirit? As Heaven's Power was not separated from the trembling of the earth, so neither will the new era of peace begin for either the Church or the world, until our hearts have been shaken and all the rocks of our pride and selfishness split and rent asunder!

If the hour is at hand for the trembling of the land, so is the Day of Triumph. The Devil has his hour, but God has His Day! The Church never has its Good Friday without its Easter Sunday. The Church is born in tragedy and defeat, and its Head is He Who found His way out of a tomb! The day is not far off when the Lily of the King shall bloom on another Easter, and those who thought it was finished, will be asked by angels: "Why are you looking for the living among the dead?" "When the nations lie in blood and their kings are a broken brood, His Feet shall be seen coming to us on the waters."

They call Christ a Deceiver! That He is! Only a Deceiver like Christ can please us, for we have already been deceived. The world is our first deceiver! It promised us peace and gave us war; it promised us enduring love and gave us age and satiety!

Come then, O Christ, our other Deceiver, You seem so stern, so hard, for You are "purpureal robed and cypress crowned." You seem to crucify our flesh and our Eros. At first glance, we shrink from You saying: "Must all Thy fields be dunged with rotten death?" But oh! What sweet deceit, for as we come to know You, we find in You that love we sought for, when the world worked on us its first deceit!

Heavenly Traitor! that seemed so dead and yet are the Risen Life! Deceive us with Your Scars — "that our weak souls might break free, and throw us back to Thee!"

Happy Easter and God love you!

P. Jorge *unclear*
2010

ST PAULS

This book was produced by St. Pauls/Alba House, the Society of St. Paul, an international religious congregation of priests and brothers dedicated to serving the Church through the communications media.

For information regarding this and associated ministries of the Pauline Family of Congregations, write to the Vocation Director, Society of St. Paul, P.O. Box 189, 9531 Akron-Canfield Road, Canfield, Ohio 44406-0189. Phone (330) 702-0359; or E-mail: spvocationoffice@aol.com or check our internet site, www.albahouse.org